THE ROOF TILE OF TEMPYŌ

THE
ROOF TILE OF
TEMPYŌ

by YASUSHI INOUÉ
translated by JAMES T. ARAKI

UNIVERSITY OF TOKYO PRESS

UNESCO COLLECTION OF REPRESENTATIVE WORKS:
JAPANESE SERIES

This book has been accepted in the Japanese Series of
the Translations Collection of the United Nations Edu-
cational, Scientific and Cultural Organization (UNESCO)

Translated from
the Japanese original *Tempyō no iraka*

© Yasushi Inoué
Published in English in Japan by arrangement with
Orion Press
English translation © 1975 by UNESCO
First paperback printing, with corrections, 1981
1991   5 4 3

Published by
UNIVERSITY OF TOKYO PRESS
ISBN 4-13-087040-8
ISBN 0-86008-307-1
Printed in Japan

Contents

Translator's Introduction

The Roof Tile of Tempyō, a historical novel for which Yasushi Inoué received the Japanese Ministry of Education Prize
in 1958, is regarded as a modern classic in Japan. Although it
is considered a historical novel in Japan, "artistic historical
narrative" would be a more appropriate designation, as it
is essentially a poetic view of the past. It is Inoué's retelling
of a dramatic episode in history rather than fiction written
with an eye to dramatic structure or detailed characterization—an ostensibly authentic narrative that focuses on the
era of Tempyō ("Heavenly Calm"), the early eighth century,
when Japan was engaged in her first attempt to acquire
the culture of an advanced civilization, the T'ang Empire
of China.

Against a backdrop encompassing most of eastern Asia, the
author focuses on four young Japanese Buddhist monks who
set sail on a perilous voyage for the Asian mainland, each
with different hopes and apprehensions. Fushō and one other
have been entrusted with the task of bringing to Japan a
learned Chinese Buddhist who can introduce orthodox monastic practices. The eminent monk Ganjin (Chien-chen in
Chinese) of Yang-chou is the one persuaded to cross the dark
green expanse to the island empire. Elements of suspense
and causality enter into the story, but the plot is basically
that provided by *The Record of the Eastward Journey of the
Great Monk of T'ang*, a terse account of Ganjin's travels recorded some years after his death by a disciple.

Through skillful linking of historic episodes, the author
brings many of the renowned figures from the eighth
century into his scenes. Among them are perhaps the most
illustrious of Chinese monarchs, Emperor Hsüan-tsung, the
fabled pirate Feng Jo-feng, who was a scourge to Persians
sailing argosies bound for Canton, and Abé Nakamaro, the
famed Japanese poet and scholar in the court of the Chinese
sovereign. The author's main concern throughout, however,
is the inner struggles, the triumphs and failures of the less
significant men among the thousands who risked their lives
to visit the T'ang empire during this phase in the growth
of Japanese civilization.

Inoué develops two motifs in presenting the broad theme of the role of transculturation in the development of Japanese civilization: one, the persistence of the venerable Chinese monk Ganjin, whose indomitable will nourishes the Japanese hope for the eventual eastward spread of Buddhist orthodoxy; the other, the significance of a lifetime of work by an aging Japanese monk, Gōgyō, who dreams of transcribing all of the important Buddhist texts in China for transmission to Japan. The latter story suggests the same pathos that marks many of Inoué's novels and short stories on historical themes—pathos born of the realization that the tasks and ideals to which men dedicate their lives seldom create so much as an eddy in the broad flow of time and history.

In telling his story, the author favors a controlled narrative with a minimum of dialogue, and he exercises considerable restraint in his historical re-creations. The narrative is straightforward, at times blunt, often with the directness of descriptive reporting. The lyrical quality, which has also become a mark of Inoué's writing, is generally absent here. Only toward the end of the story, when the author ponders the probable fate of Gōgyō and his lifework, does he favor an imaginative passage, rich in imagery, in order to bring the story to a sudden, effectively lyrical climax.

In writing *The Roof Tile of Tempyō*, Inoué strove to remain faithful to the historical record and to refrain from enlarging imaginatively upon thematic material. Perhaps for this reason a number of intriguing motifs are never developed, nor are his characterizations unfolded completely as in his novels on contemporary themes. An exception is the characterization of Ganjin, which is precise and finely drawn. In this instance the author was guided by an authentic likeness sculpted in Ganjin's time, and he relied on his intuition as a novelist to breathe life into the statue. When Inoué has ample historical material upon which to draw, he can bring his characters into relief with stunning effect. An admirable example of this is his *Emperor-Abdicate Shirakawa II* (1972), a portrait of a medieval Japanese sovereign. Four close observers had kept detailed diaries of the same aspects of the monarch's personality at different stages in his life, and from

their records and from chronicles and histories of the era
Inoué fashioned the viewpoints of the four.

Some of our own novelists have used a similar approach in
writing historical novels, although seldom as scrupulously as
Inoué. "Whenever surviving records are meagre," Robert
Graves writes in his foreword to *Count Belisarius*, "I have
been obliged to fill in the gaps of the story with fiction, but
have usually had a historical equivalent in mind; so that if
exactly this or that did not happen, something similiar probably did."

Both Graves and Inoué have experimented with various
blends of historical authenticity and imaginative reconstruction. The classical setting, whether Rome or Japan, will
impose some conformity on diction and, possibly, tone. But
poetic sensibility, which they share, may explain why readers are drawn rather consistently to the isolated, often lonely,
at times idealistic figures like the Count of *Count Belisarius*
or Claudius and Germanicus of *I, Claudius*; the intensely
human sovereigns of Korea portrayed by Inoué in *Wind and
Waves* (1963), or Shinzei in *Shirakawa II*, the Buddhist statesman whom Japanese historians have tended to treat unkindly,
and certainly Gōgyō and Fushō of the present volume.

The reader of *The Roof Tile of Tempyō*, however, will be
increasingly impressed by its contrast with his total reading
experience. He will find few of the usual ingredients of an
excitingly imaginative story. In *Count Belisarius*, the pitch of
interest is heightened by vivid descriptions of the tactics and
strategy of war, raids, plunder and rape, and moments of
triumph and glorification. *I, Claudius* is replete with similar
descriptions of political intrigue, carnage in palaces and
arenas, and bacchanalian orgies. Inoué has written historical
novels that contain many of those ingredients. But *The Roof
Tile of Tempyō* is not a work written in the author's usual
mode of fiction; absence of plot in the ordinary sense
immediately sets it apart. We may consider it a pure embod-
iment of Inoué's individual approach to the art of storytelling—an approach influenced by his humanity and his
sensitivity to the traditional values and attitudes of his own
society. Confucian ethics and dignity, a Buddhist sense of

lonely serenity, forebearance, and resignation are aspects of the Japanese that often set the tone of his stories, and they are much in evidence in this novel. Passions that run stark and unbridled would be as much out of place in his novels as they would be in the traditional Japanese household. Inoué has, of course, often treated violence and sex, but he is apt to dwell on their implications or significance—as he did in *Hunting Gun* (1950).

As *The Roof Tile of Tempyō* unfolds, Inoué is at all times both storyteller and historian. Had he chosen to draw the reader into an altogether illusory world in historical time, he might have had Fushō function as the narrator. First-person narrative is conducive to subjective commentary and facilitates fictional elaboration; we find this effectively exemplified in Graves's stories and in the novels of Mary Renault. What Inoué has striven to establish is historical authenticity, and the results have been well received by discriminating Japanese readers, who usually relegate more imaginative re-creations —equivalents of our historical romances—to the less estimable Japanese category of "popular" fiction.

For the most part the author tells the story as it might have been related by Fushō, but frequently he retreats from the time setting to describe episodes or to comment on history in retrospect. Abrupt chronological shifts from past to present, or from one point in the past to another, are not so conspicuous or awkward in Japanese, in which there are only two basic tense forms.

The Japanese reader is quite comfortable viewing the past occasionally from the vantage point of the twentieth century. He will recognize, as such, documented legends, miracles and folk beliefs, as well as portents, omens, and miracles, with which the author has embellished a fabric of verified historical information; such imaginative accounts are not modified so as to appear logically feasible, nor are they assimilated into the texture of the story as they are, for instance, in *Hercules, My Shipmate*, Graves's tale about the Argonauts' voyage in quest of the golden fleece, or Mary Renault's distinguished pair of novels centering upon the legend of Theseus and the Minotaur. Among the deeply rooted Asian assumptions about dreams is the belief that dreams anticipate the future or that they provide the souls of living persons with instant passage to points infinitely removed. The inclusion of an episode based on such a belief may enhance a historical novel in the Asian tradition, whereas it would surely be considered a flaw in comparable works in the Western tradition of historical novels (dating back, say, to the works of Sir Walter Scott). This is but one example of differences in literary technique.

Qualities that give *The Roof Tile of Tempyō* distinction, insofar as Japanese readers are concerned, are those which to us will seem characteristically Japanese. The intellectual growth of the Japanese during the Era of Tempyō, the venturesome excursions by an insular people into a new geographical and religious realm, the process of cultural borrowing from the T'ang empire, the influence on their own lives and outlook—these are topics most attractive to the Japanese reader, whose present-day society has not yet fully assimilated the largesse of a second great cultural incursion from the perplexingly "modern" world of the West. The name of T'ang retains its magic in Japan, and the informed reader sees dramatic significance even in the mere itemization of products of the T'ang empire during its efflorescence. Western students have been fascinated by similar though more fully described itemizations in Edward H. Schafer's study of T'ang culture, *The Golden Peaches of Samarkand* (1963).

The author introduces names that will not enhance the dramatic value of the narrative for the Western reader. The convention of providing the reader with fleeting glimpses of people is considered an especially agreeable one in Japanese historical fiction. Most Japanese readers take considerable satisfaction in recognizing Yang Kuei-fei, the most celebrated beauty in Chinese history, An Lu-shan, the red-bearded general whose rebellion brought an end to a golden age, statesmen, poets, and calligraphers of China and Japan whom they know from history and literature.

As in all forms of traditional Japanese literature, due emphasis is given to nature and the seasons and to the responses they have traditionally inspired. The astute reader will recognize conventional poetic images. Furthermore, the general character of the human figures in the novel—their

outlook, taciturn nature, contemplative attitude, the contradiction between an emotion and its manifestation—appeals
to the contemporary Japanese. Nowhere is this in greater
evidence than in the final chapter, when the deeper significance of the roof tile is perceived by Fushō, who, typically,
does not translate his perception into words. The old, damaged roof tile may itself be seen as a symbol of the decline of
T'ang civilization and of Buddhism in China. In its transmission to Japan and in the preservation of its form in a monastery the reader sees the symbolic expression of the ascendance
in Japan of the Buddhist vehicle, already beginning to decline
and soon to be proscribed in China.

Among other features that enhance the story, though they
may puzzle the Western reader, are the constant references to
the ages of the characters, a device in Japanese biographical
writing that the author seems to have employed purposely to
achieve the effect of authentic chronicling; the repetition of
names of cities and monasteries in China, which will not be
tedious for the reader of Japanese, who enjoys gaining visual
familiarity with names written elegantly and meaningfully
in Chinese graphs (the name Lung-hsing-ssu, for example,
will be recognized immediately for its semantic value of
"dragon-rising monastery"); the occasional recapitulation of
previous events, a storytelling device more common to the
epic narrative than the modern dramatic novel, which the
author may have found useful in writing and publishing this
novel in serial form.

Prose style is an important consideration in the Japanese
assessment of this novel. *The Roof Tile of Tempyō* is not an
easy novel for most Japanese to read. The rich variety of
Chinese graphs lends to the author's style a quality of erudition which echoes that which is most attractive about traditional scholarly prose, and it is consistent with the subject
matter and the setting. Nowhere does one encounter such
things as mid-twentieth century English slang spouted by
Romans of the fourth century as in Evelyn Waugh's *Helena*
(by Waugh's purposeful design, of course). Chinese graphs
have a visually aesthetic import and are often combined into
digraphs that may impart a particular acuteness of meaning,

an added overtone or implication, or heightened imagery, but these are often lost in translation.

Many of the conventions described above are accepted ones in the Chinese literary tradition. China has, in fact, adopted *The Roof Tile of Tempyō* in Chinese translation as an expression of her own cultural heritage. Chou En-lai several years ago acclaimed the novel implicitly by feting Inoué and making certain he could, on that occasion, refer to the novel by its original Japanese title, *Tempyō no iraka*. In any event, the fame of Ganjin, a man long forgotten in China, has been resurrected in the region of Yang-chou, where he had lived and preached twelve centuries before.

In Japan, *The Roof Tile of Tempyō* has been analyzed exhaustively by persons determined to isolate fact from fiction; such miracles depicted in the story as the heaven-sent rain of nectar have been scientifically explained. More important, the book has been much discussed for its value as historical narrative and its significance as literature that presents truths beyond the mere facts of history.

Having been apprised of the subtleties in the original, of its curiously non-Western characteristics, and of the literary and cultural criteria by which the Japanese have evaluated the novel, the Western reader may wish to try to share the experience of a Japanese reading the original. *The Roof Tile of Tempyō* is a novel typical of many that have garnered praise within Japan but are considered too "Japanese" for successful introduction to a Western audience. It is hoped that this reading experience will provide passage to an area of the Japanese literary taste that has seldom been made accessible to readers outside East Asia.

About the Author

Yasushi Inoué was born in 1907 in a small town in Hokkaido, northernmost of the Japanese isles. The son of an army medical officer, he spent much of his childhood with his grandmother at the family home in the rural interior of Izu Peninsula, not far from Mount Fuji, while his parents moved about from one military post to another. He attended high school in the city of Kanazawa on the coast of the Japan Sea where his parents had settled during this period. His principal interests during those few years were jujitsu and poetry. He spent his first adult years in idyllic freedom, reading avidly and contributing to literary activities in Tokyo, before resuming his formal education. He was in his late twenties when he graduated from Kyoto Imperial University in 1936 with a bachelor's degree in aesthetics.

A literary career seemed to be in the offing for the young Inoué, whose writings during his student days had won immediate recognition. His *Moon of Meiji* had already been published and then staged by a reputable troupe, and his first short story had won a minor contest sponsored by the newspaper *Mainichi Shimbun*. Instead, he went to work for the *Mainichi* and remained a professional newspaperman for the next dozen years, except for a half-year spent as a foot soldier, most of it marching with pack horses about the plains of north China.

In the chaotic postwar society of Japan, Inoué found the subject for *The Bull Fight*, a novel which earned him the coveted Akutagawa Prize in 1950. A fledgling author at forty-three, he relinquished the opportunity to occupy an executive desk and entered upon a new career of professional writing. Another instant success, published almost simultaneously with *The Bull Fight*, was *Hunting Gun*, a short novel on a contemporary psychological theme. During that year, Inoué published more than a dozen short stories, an anthology of poetry, and two full-length novels. One of the novels, *Black Tide*, was a dramatization of the mystery surrounding the death of a prominent public figure; it contributed to and encouraged the vogue in Japan for novelistic treatment of contemporary social and political events.

Poetry, Japanese literary critics have often written, is the source of many of Inoué's stories. *Hunting Gun*, for example, is an imaginative expansion of a prose poem of the same title he had composed earlier. More than once Inoué has employed prose fiction as a means of magnifying and extending an impression, perception, or image that may originally have inspired a poem. The entire story of the *Counterfeiter* may well have been created to serve as an extended introduction to an earlier poem, "Man's Lifetime"—the unforgettable image of a withered old man setting off fireworks that blossom in the night sky to the delight of the crowd, but who is himself so preoccupied with the rapid firing that he can never have a glimpse of the beauty of his own invention.

Many of Inoué's novels in the popular vein are directed at the newspaper and magazine reader, but even in these efforts he strives to maintain a high level of artistry. The work that led to his candidacy for the Academy of Arts Prize, which he received in 1959, was a novel about a love triangle, *The Ice Cliff*, which was first published in two hundred and seventy daily installments in the *Asahi Shimbun*. Inoué's ability to write artistic autobiographical prose as well was generally recognized in "Light of the Moon" (1969), a portrait of his aging mother.

During the past fifteen years, Inoué has focused more and more on the historical novel. He followed his initial success, *The Roof Tile of Tempyō*, with *Lou-lan* (1958), *Tun-huang* (1959), and *The Blue Wolf* (1959), the last a partly fictional biography of Genghis Khan; these novels take the reader back in history to dramas that once unfolded on the central Asian plains. *The Diary of Lady Yodo* (1961), historical fiction of a more imaginative and popular variety, traces the turbulent career of the consort of the warrior Hideyoshi, and earned the author the Noma Literary Prize. In 1964, Inoué was elected to membership in the Academy of Arts of Japan and, in the same year, received the Yomiuri Newspaper Prize for his *Wind and Waves*, a poignant, historically faithful portrayal of the kingdom of Korea, once the hapless instrument of Kublai Khan's attempt to conquer Japan. He was selected as the first recipient, in 1969, of the Japanese Literature Grand Prize in recognition of his *A Bemusing Tale about Russia* (1967), which describes the adventures of shipwrecked Japanese who wander far into the Siberian continent, one of them traveling as far as St. Petersburg, during the eighteenth century.

Inoué has been a remarkably prolific writer through the years, and there has been little diminution in his writing energy. But he now tends to select his subject matter with greater care. His preparatory research displays the high quality and thoroughness of professional scholarship. His

Journey Beyond Samarkand (English edition, 1971) was born of visits to Central Asia and exhaustive study of ancient literary and historical documents and recent research by Russian archaeologists.

During the summer of 1967, Inoué lectured at the University of Hawaii as Scholar in Residence. He is currently working on *Wadatsumi*, a historical novel of epic proportions on the theme of Japanese migration to the United States.

Other books available in English by Inoué include *The Hunting Gun*, *The Counterfeiter* (with other stories), *Journey Beyond Samarkand*, and *The Azaleas of Hira* (also with other stories).

About the Translation

The single-volume Japanese edition of the novel is divided into five long chapters. The twenty-one sections of the translation provide an approximation of the structure of the novel as it originally appeared in serial form. Parenthetical explanations in the translation are those given by the author in the original text. Additional explanations, supplied by the translator in footnotes, are equivalent to the descriptive notes that are appended to most Japanese editions of the novel.

The lunar months have been changed to their approximate solar-calendric equivalents (the first month as January, the second as February, and so on), although in terms of the seasons the first lunar month would correspond more closely to February. Because the lunar month consisted of thirty days or less, an intercalary month was added periodically in order to keep the months and the seasons in agreement. In a year with thirteen months, one of the months occurred twice; March, for instance, was followed by the intercalary month of March. The ages of characters have been adjusted to agree with ages calculated by Western reckoning.

Names have been rendered as they are in China and Japan, with the surname first. The Japanese pronunciations of Ganjin and Zen (Ch'an in Chinese) have been used throughout. Titles of Indian Buddhist texts have usually been rendered in Sanscrit; titles of Chinese and Japanese origin have in general been translated. The Buddhist name Gōgyō may also be read as Gyōgō or Gyōkō.

The text used for the translation was published by Shinchosha in 1972. I am indebted to the author, who kindly corrected the typographical errors in the Japanese edition, and to my friend Rita Gay Oldham and my student James H. Shields for invaluable suggestions regarding the translation.

James T. Araki

THE ROOF TILE OF TEMPYŌ

Prologue

During the reign of Emperor Shōmu, the imperial government decided to send the ninth ambassadorial mission to the T'ang court. The year was 732, the fourth year of the Tempyō era. On the seventeenth of August, appointments were made to the posts of the Four Offices of the Embassy to T'ang. Tajihi Hironari, a courtier of the fourth rank, was designated ambassador, and Nakatomi Nashiro, who held the fifth rank, was named vice-ambassador. Hata Asamoto and three others were assigned to the office of praetor, and four others were assigned to the office of scribe. In September emissaries were dispatched from the court to the provinces of Ōmi, Tamba, Harima, and Aki, bearing orders for the construction of a ship in each of these provinces.

Ambassador-elect Hironari was the fifth son of Tajihi Shima, Minister of the Left at the court of Emperor Mommu.* Hironari's elder brother, Agatamori, had headed the ambassadorial mission sent fifteen years before to the T'ang court. Now, Hironari, who had served as governor of Shimotsuké Province, as assistant commander of guards at the embassy of the Korean kingdom of Silla, and as governor of Echizen Province, was to assume this office of greater distinction and responsibility. The vice-ambassador Nakatomi Nashiro's father, Shimamaro, was the grandson of Nakatomi Tarumé, brother of the illustrious Nakatomi Kamatari.†

Besides the principal officers, already selected and formally appointed, such missions usually included shipmasters, Shinto priests, physicians, astrologers, diviners, artists, and interpreters of Chinese, Korean, and Ryukyuan, as well as navigators, carpenters, metal workers, chief oarsmen, chant masters and chanters,† overseers, jade workers, founders, craftsmen, and shipwrights. Including the usual complement of oarsmen and archers, more than five hundred and eighty persons would be on board the four vessels.

*Reigned 697–707.

†Kamatari played the major role in the restoration, in 645, of the political primacy to the imperial clan. His descendants, surnamed Fujiwara, dominated the court for many centuries.

†The chanters may have performed the task of raising choruses of shouts to repel oncoming waves during storms.

The process of selecting students to go to China, however, could not be completed and was carried over into the following year. The Japanese sent missions to the T'ang empire primarily to enable young scholars and Buddhist monks to study there. The government's interest in the religion and culture of China had led to the expenditure of vast sums to dispatch these missions, notwithstanding the risk to many lives; what political motive there may have been was of little importance. The tiny island empire was affected in some way by every change in the fortunes of nations on the continent and the Korean Peninsula. The Japanese at the time considered their most crucial, self-imposed problem to be the achievement of modern statehood as quickly as possible. Although less than ninety years had passed since Prince Naka-no-ōe had guided Japan into a system of codes and laws, and but one hundred and eighty since the introduction of Buddhism, the system of government and other aspects of culture were already deeply inbued with influences from the Asian mainland. But the borrowings had not coalesced in a meaningful way. The Japanese had established merely the outlines of a national state. There remained much to be acquired from the more advanced civilization of China. In terms of growth, Japan was somewhere between childhood and youth. In terms of the seasons she was just entering the month of March, when the first faint warmth of the oncoming spring has begun to pervade the still frigid atmosphere.

The city of Nara had been the nation's capital for twenty-three years. To the Japanese it was an impressive copy of Ch'ang-an, the capital of the T'ang empire; it contained nine great avenues running east and west, intersected by an equal number of major streets running north and south. But the outskirts of the city had already become a gathering place for vagrants. More than forty Buddhist monasteries had been erected. Among them were Kōfuku-ji, Daian-ji, Gangō-ji, Yakushi-ji, Katsuragi-dera, and Ki-no-tera.* Despite all their magnificence, the clustered monastery buildings betrayed an emptiness, for only a few sutras were to be found in the repositories of sacred texts.

*The suffixes *ji, dera,* and *tera* denote "monastery."

With the arrival of the new year, nine devout Buddhist monks, chosen from among many throughout the nation, were sent to the Shinto shrines of Kashii, Munakata, and Aso, to the state Buddhist monasteries, and to the Shinto-Buddhist temples.* There they prayed for the success of the forthcoming voyage to China. In order to quell the wrath of the sea god, the *Sutra of the Dragon King* was recited in the five home provinces as well as in the seven districts in the outer reaches of the empire. Court emissaries made offerings at Grand Isé and at other Shinto shrines throughout the country.

1

In early February the Buddhist monks Fushō and Yōei were offered the opportunity to go to China to study. They had not expected such a distinction and were surprised when they were summoned to Gankō-ji by Ryūson, reputedly the most influential monk in the Buddhist hierarchy, and asked if they would like to study in China. Neither had talked informally with Ryūson before, although they had attended his lectures on the *Avataṃsaka Sūtra*. Ordinarily they would not be able to meet with a person of such high rank.

Yōei was large and roughhewn, with somewhat rounded shoulders. His face was seldom clean-shaven. Though he was in his early thirties, he could be mistaken for a man ten years older. Fushō, much smaller and frail, was a few years younger.

Yōei answered immediately that he would accept the proposal. The tone of his reply suggested that he was accommodating Ryūson. Fushō, however, took a while to answer. Peering somewhat timidly into Ryūson's face, he asked him what he might be expected to study in China. Fushō doubtless considered this a reasonable question, for he did not think that his ability to learn would be enhanced by a change in geographical location. He saw no purpose in risking his life in order to get to China. These thoughts could almost be read in his small eyes, which seemed to reflect cold indif-

*The Japanese worshiped both Shinto and Buddhist deities. This eclecticism is reflected in the Shinto-Buddhist temples (*jingū-ji*), Buddhist sanctuaries built on the grounds of Shinto shrines.

ference. Looked upon as the most promising among the younger "prodigies," he was contemptuous of the role; he regarded himself as a hardworking monk who seldom left his study desk.

Ryūson spoke in his customary subdued manner to the two quite different young monks. In Japan, he explained to them, Buddhist ordination rituals were not being properly observed, and so he wished to have a qualified master brought from China to administer monastic vows. To invite a qualified teacher sounded simple enough, he continued, but it was a task of persuasion that would require years of effort. Such a teacher must be a person of unquestioned scholarly and moral attainment, and it would be no easy matter to induce him to leave his native country. It would be at least fifteen years before another Japanese embassy could be sent to the T'ang court, and by then the two monks, working together, should be able to accomplish this task.

Fushō was amazed that so many years would have to be devoted to bringing back a Buddhist who could transmit the monastic rites to Japan. He realized, however, that he and Yōei would have to be competent to make a wise selection. Furthermore, in the course of negotiations their personalities must influence the man they were trying to attract. They would surely have to spend a dozen or more years in the T'ang empire before they could attempt to fulfill the task. This was what Ryūson was trying to explain.

Fushō accepted because it gave him the opportunity to live all of fifteen years in the T'ang empire. He would have been reluctant to gamble his life on a voyage taking him to China for only a few years; but he would risk a voyage, though it promised almost certain peril, for the rewards of an extended stay.

After taking leave of Ryūson, the two monks walked to Kōfuku-ji and lingered a while on the sun-dappled grounds. They talked about the unexpected turn of events. A flame of excitement had been kindled in Yōei, and he talked rapidly. He felt certain, he said, his name had been brought up during consultations between Ryūson and the minister of state Prince Toneri.

At the time, peasants oppressed by corvée and taxation

*reason
for ordination*

Sōniryō

punishment

were deserting the village in droves and becoming vagrants or finding refuge in the clergy. For several decades the government had tried to stop this trend by enacting dozens of new laws, but all attempts were futile. The degradation of Buddhist monks and nuns was an equally distressing problem to the government. The "Twenty-seven Articles," designating qualifications for ranks within the clergy, had been proclaimed some years earlier, but this proclamation was ineffectual. Buddhists had no set precepts to follow; furthermore the Supreme Clerical Vow* was not being administered for lack of the requisite three masters and seven attestors (the ten monks who conduct the ritual). Consequently, monks and nuns were self-ordained or, at best, merely took the vow to abide by the three ideal precepts, and there were no effective restraints against license. The errant Buddhists could be regulated if an orthodox system of ordination were instituted by an eminent monk from the T'ang empire. Man's laws having failed, there remained no recourse other than turning to the teachings of Śākya Buddha. Obviously the need to institute orthodox ordination was an urgent one. These considerations underlay the decision of Prince Toneri and Ryūson to dispatch the two young monks abroad.

"This mission would certainly be worth staking our lives on, wouldn't you say?" Yōei remarked to Fushō.

Fushō did not answer. His thoughts, as always, were centered on himself. What significance would there be in bringing a teacher of monastic discipline to Japan? The question did not interest him. But how many of the sacred writings would he be able to study during those fifteen years? This question excited him. He felt as if the mass of the scriptures were pressing down on him, and the sensation lent a feverish glow to his normally cold eyes.

"Yōei: born in Mino Province; family history unknown; served as a resident monk at Kōfuku-ji; a man of great erudition, known to be peerless in debate; a specialist in the *yoga* and *vijñana-matravāda*." This, recorded in the ninth-century *Enryaku Era Directory of Buddhist Monks*, is the only informa-

---

*The vow to observe moral precepts—more than two hundred for monks, more than three hundred for nuns. The number varied with the sect.

tion available on Yōei prior to his departure for the T'ang empire. There is even less information on Fushō—one vague item, stating that he was a monk who had served at either the Kōfuku-ji or Daian-ji. The *Second Chronicle of Japan*, a history compiled in 797, however, contains an entry for the eighth of February, 766, that throws light on an area of his background: "Eighth day: Shirai Yoroshimé was promoted to the junior fifth rank, lower grade; she is the mother of Fushō, the monk-scholar who went to China for studies." Thus we know that Fushō's mother, Yoroshimé, was a member of the Shirai clan, and that she was promoted from the sixth to the fifth court rank. The Shirai clan was descended from a nephew of King Chin-ŏ of the Korean kingdom of Paikche, and many of the clan's members were active in foreign diplomacy; these are facts known to history.

On the twenty-sixth of the intercalary month of March, the ambassador-elect Hironari was granted an audience by the Emperor and awarded the ambassadorial sword. The sword was to be restored to the palace upon Hironari's return to Japan. Its bestowal signified that preparations for the voyage had been completed, that the recipient was granted full authority as Japan's ambassador to the T'ang court, and that the ships would weigh anchor at the first sign of fair weather.

At the beginning of the month Hironari had paid a visit to Yamanoué Okura, a courtier who had been in China as a scribe for the seventh mission, dispatched to the T'ang empire in 702. The fact that Okura had experienced a voyage to China and, moreover, was an intimate friend of his elder brother might have been the reason the new ambassador favored him with this courteous gesture. Okura, to honor the occasion, dedicated a poem and two envois to Hironari:

> Since the age of the *kami** it has been said
> That Yamato, whose mountains fill the sky,
> Is a majestic land of the imperial *kami*,
> A land blest by the mana of words.
> It has been so retold
> From mouth to mouth, age to age.

*Deities of the pantheon of Japanese Shinto.

9 The Roof Tile of Tempyō

All of us, living today, see and know it.
Though worthy men are many,
The Mikado of the High-Radiant Sun, divine,
Out of fond affection,
Has chosen you, a scion of a minister's house.
You have received his solemn command,
And to the far-off land of China
You will be sent, and you will go.
The *kami* who dwell by the shores and in the deep
Of the expanse that is their domain—
The great, exalted *kami*—
Will guide you at the prow.
The great, exalted *kami* of heaven and earth
And the Spirit of the Great Land of Yamato
Will wing about the heavens and scan the expanse
From distant celestial heights.
When you return, your duties done,
The great, exalted *kami* shall, again,
Lay their hands on the prow
And speed you along a course,
Straight and direct as an ink line,
From the cape of yonder-lying Chika to Ōtomo,
To the shore of Mitsu, where your ship will moor.
Fare well, let there be no mischance.
Come back quickly!

　　I shall await you
In Ōtomo at the pine grove
　　Of Mitsu, its sand
Swept clean by my broom.
Come back quickly!

　　I shall hear
Of your ship casting anchor
　　At Naniwa Bay;
Then will I untie my waistband
And hasten to your side.

The latter envoi was dedicated to Hironari's wife, who would
be keeping vigil during her husband's absence.

At dawn on the third of April Hironari's party departed from Nara for the bay of Naniwa.* Most members of the mission were already at the port. The party that left Nara on horseback that day comprised only thirty men, Fushō and Yōei among them. As they rode, the tolling of numerous temple bells wished them safe passage. Although it was spring, the petals of the cherry blossoms were still tightly folded, and the breeze at daybreak bore the chill of mid-winter.

The travelers took the road crossing the Yamato Plain and, continuing northwest through Ōji and over Tatsuta Mountain, they reached the administrative center of the province and took lodging for the night. Shortly before noon the next day they arrived at Naniwa, site of a former capital. The construction of an imperial detached palace, begun nine years before, was still in progress, and here and there homes were being built for members of the court. Having made their way through several construction sites that basked in the whitish rays of the spring sun, they entered the shop-lined streets of the commercial section. They crossed several bridges. The moment they crossed the last, they felt the salt-laden wind that blew in from the sea. On a hillside to their left stood Naniwa Mansion, resplendent in a new coat of vermilion and green paint, and beyond it, the Koguryō Embassy, the Paikche Embassy, and the Silla Embassy†— aged and forgotten despite their illustrious names. A section of the harbor, under a cover of reeds, was visible beyond the rise ahead of them.

The party was soon at the port. There were few traces of the era when Naniwa flourished as the center of thriving commerce with the three kingdoms of Korea. Even so, a forest of masts, hundreds of them, soared up above the reeds. The port lay at the estuary of a convergence of several rivers. Islets and sandbars of all shapes and sizes dotted the broad expanse where the incoming tide met the flow of fresh water. Ships entering the port had to thread their way through this maze of islets and sandbars; from land they appeared to be

*Today, the general area of Osaka city.
†Koguryō, Paikche, and Silla were the three independent kingdoms of Korea until 675, when Silla succeeded in unifying the peninsula.

gliding through reeds. Many guideposts projected out of the
reeds, and the small white birds perched on them seemed to
glitter in the eyes of those who would that day depart for an
unknown and distant land.

The docking area was alive with activity. Four large vessels
were moored some distance from the shore, where a large
crowd had gathered. Only the families of those departing
were allowed on the landing. There might have been as many
as two thousand people, among them women, young and
old, and children too. The throng outside the dock was even
larger, and vagabonds and beggars wandered in its midst.
From time to time the chanting of Buddhist sutras and Shinto
prayers was heard over the din and confusion on the docks.

> When hoarfrost falls
> On the moor where travelers
> Seek shelter for repose,
> Enfold my child with your wings,
> O flock of cranes of heaven!

This poem, in the ninth book of *A Collection of a Myriad
Leaves*,* was composed by a woman who had come to see
her only child board one of the ships bound for the T'ang
empire. There is another, in the eighth book, composed by
the courtier Kasa Kanamura and presented on that day to
the ambassador to T'ang China:

> Beyond the waves
> A small island vanishes
> Behind the clouds.
> Were we to be so parted,
> Oh, the choking grief!

This poem, however, would have been appropriate for a
woman coming to bid her husband farewell. Surely Kasa
Kanamura had composed it on behalf of an acquaintance.

The thirty men of Ambassador Hironari's party, who had
left the capital the morning before, were at the edge of the
dock, paying their respects to well-wishers. Formalities com-

*The first anthology of Japanese poetry, compiled in 759.

pleted, the men went aboard ships, where they toasted one
another with wine cups filled with water, as was customary
before embarking on a perilous venture.

The four ships were large, measuring fifty yards in length
and about four yards in width, and each could provide ample
space for as many as one hundred and forty voyagers. Perhaps
because the ships had been built in different provinces, each
was shaped distinctively. The lead vessel, which carried Ambassador Hironari, was broad amidships. The second, with
the vice-ambassador aboard, was narrower; it also differed
from the lead ship in the shape and location of its superstructure. The third and fourth, on which the praetors would
be sailing, were moored side by side, their sterns presenting
a striking contrast in appearance. The stern of the third ship
arched magnificently, towering a good six feet above that
of the vessel alongside.

No one could judge whether the craft he boarded would
be more seaworthy than the others. Not even the directors
of the commission charged with the construction could tell,
nor could the shipwrights of Ōmi, Tamba, Harima, and Aki
provinces, who had shaped the planks. The four vessels were
alike in only one respect: the mast of each was mounted
amidships, as was customary with the vessels of Paikche,
rather than off-center, which was usual in Chinese vessels.
Shipwrights seemed to place more reliance on the crafts of
Paikche, with which Japan had maintained close ties since
early history.

The four great vessels waited for the incoming tide, and
at dusk left the docks of Naniwa. Once away from the banks,
they appeared so ponderous that onlookers wondered whether they might not tip over and sink into the reeds. Every
vessel was laden beyond capacity with some one hundred
and fifty persons and cargo that included food, clothing, and
medicine as well as commodities to provide revenue for
passengers during their stay abroad, and a vast load of goods
to be presented to the T'ang imperial court. A great roar
arose from the well-wishers as the ships were leaving the bank;
then all fell quiet. Two hours elapsed before the last of the
four vessels sailed out of the bay.

2

The four ships left Naniwa on the fourth of April, touched at various points along the coast of the Inland Sea, and arrived at the bay of Ōtsu in Kyushu about the middle of the month. They lay idle for several days, awaiting a favorable wind, at this last Japanese port of call. Near the end of April, more than a month after Hironari had accepted the ambassadorial sword, the ships left Ōtsu and headed for the open sea.

There were two sea routes the Japanese could take from the bay of Ōtsu to China. The first five missions, the last of which was sent during the reign of Emperor Tenji,* touched at the islands of Iki and Tsushima and then sailed north, along the southwest coast of Korea, and across the mouth of the Gulf of Pohai. The parties landed at either Lai-chou or Teng-chou on the Shantung Peninsula, from where they traveled southwest to Lo-yang and then to Ch'ang-an. This route was safe as long as southern Korea was within Japan's sphere of influence. Following the unification of the Korean Peninsula by the kingdom of Silla, the Japanese were compelled to find another route. The next three missions, sent between 702 and 717, sailed west from the port of Ōtsu across the Iki Strait to Chika Island, where they waited for winds that would take the ships across the East China Sea to the coast of either Yang-chou or Su-chou, both near the estuary of the Yangtze River. Hironari's party intended to take the latter route.

Yōei and Fushō were aboard the third ship, which was under the command of the praetor Hata Asamoto. Two other student-monks, Kaiyū and Genrō, were also on this vessel. Kaiyū, from Kyushu, had joined them the day they sailed from Ōtsu. He appeared to be about as old as Fushō. He was a large man, and his bearing suggested arrogance. Genrō, from Kii Province, was two or three years younger. He was said to have been at the Daian-ji during the previous year, but neither Fushō nor Yōei had ever met the young monk or, for that matter, had ever heard his name. His features were

*Reigned 661–671.

well proportioned, and his speech and bearing betokened a gentle upbringing.

From the night they left the port of Ōtsu, the ships were tossed about like so many leaves by large swells. The sea was not truly stormy, and the crew fared well, but most of the passengers soon lost all craving for food and lay quite helpless. Fushō was an exception. Although the first two days he had suffered along with the rest, after that he was free of dizziness and nausea and sat easily despite the pitching and rolling. But he was distressed to see the other three monks lying beside him, tortured by seasickness from dawn to dusk. Yōei suffered the most. Soft moans of agony issued continually from his parted lips. His face, distinguished by dark brows and alert eyes, became emaciated so quickly, it was a pity to behold. Genrō was virtually lifeless—he neither stirred nor spoke.

Late one afternoon, as darkness was beginning to settle over the water, Kaiyū, who lay on the mat farthest from Fushō, spoke to him: "What are you thinking about?"

The huge monk looked insolently at Fushō, with whom he had never before conversed. They had exchanged the customary formal greetings upon coming aboard, giving their names and home provinces, but then both had succumbed immediately to seasickness. They suffered in solitude and had no opportunity to talk. The monk from Kyushu lay sprawled on his back, staring at Fushō.

"Nothing in particular," Fushō replied.

Since their first meeting, Fushō could not conceive of this hulking monk as possessing any quality to justify his inclusion among the monks to be sent abroad to study. The man had an indefinable rustic quality—a lack of polish that might be expected of a monk from the provinces.

"I've been thinking . . ." Kaiyū said.

"Thinking what?"

". . . that suffering can only be understood by one who's suffering and by no one else, and if one is suffering, one can only face up to it the best one can because one has no other choice. I'm suffering now, and I'm not the only one. Look at Yōei, Genrō, and the rest. But you're not. Luckily you've managed to avoid it."

Fushō took offense at the remark. Yet he knew that if he had thought enough about the others, he would have realized he felt no compassion for them. He felt sorry for them, of course, but there was nothing he could do to help them; even if there had been, he would not have felt the compulsion to act. But he did not like to acknowledge his own callousness.

Kaiyū rambled on, as if he had read Fushō's thoughts. "Don't feel bad. I've simply said what's true. If we could exchange places, I'd be as you are. Men are like that."

Having said so much, Kaiyū rolled over and tried to force something up from an already empty stomach. He moaned: "Oh . . . what misery . . ."

Fushō talked occasionally with the young monk Genrō. When the ship was tossed about violently, Genrō would speak out. He seemed compelled to talk to allay his fear. His voice was so faint that at times he sounded as if he were uttering a plea, or simply muttering to himself, and yet his words were earnest.

"It's not so bad," Genrō said. "Just a little more perseverance . . . that's all. I will get to China as long as the ship doesn't founder. I'll be able to see the twin capitals, Ch'ang-an and Lo-yang. I've heard so much about them. I'll walk about and be able to think things out. I'll actually see the famous monasteries—the An-kuo-ssu, Great Tz'u-en-ssu, Hsi-ming-ssu*. . . . Surely I'll study at one of those monasteries. I've so much to learn. I've so many things to read. I'll see and hear so much, all with my own eyes and ears. I'll acquire whatever is to be acquired in the vast land of China. Only a little more perseverance . . . only a little more."

As Fushō listened, he was impressed with the strange melancholy of Genrō's words. Genrō struck a similar responsive note in all the others; his remarks touched an area of obscure apprehension that they shared but were reluctant to talk about. When he spoke, Genrō's face was ashen. The others listened in uneasy silence, as if to say: "Let him prattle if he wants to."

Just once, Kaiyū expressed his annoyance: "Stop talking

---

*The Chinese suffix *ssu*, like the Japanese *ji*, means "monastery." It also occurs, though less frequently, as a suffix designating a government office.

nonsense! We don't even know whether this ship will ever reach land again. Can't you understand that?"

Yōei never spoke. Even during tense moments, there was no telling whether he was listening to those about him. He lay sighing, staring vacantly at the sky.

Gradually all the monks were released from the agonies of seasickness, which they likened to the torments of hell. The younger they were, the sooner relief came: first, Genrō; a few days later, Kaiyū; after another few days, Yōei. Although during his sickness Genrō had spoken often of his yearning for China, when he recovered he became close-mouthed, and it was not unusual for him to be silent throughout the day. The young monk, whose delicate features and gentility set him somewhat apart, was being overtaken by an inexplicable melancholy. Kaiyū was languid and lay on his mat even though the malady had left him. Yōei recited the *Lotus Sutra* throughout the day. Fushō would occasionally cast a condescending glance at the goings-on around him as he studied the seventh scroll of the *Manual of Vinaya Sect Rituals,** which he kept at his side and intended to finish reading during the voyage.

The third ship sailed between Ambassador Hironari's lead ship and the fourth. The second had been assigned the rear position. For the twenty days following their departure from Kyushu, the monks could see the other ships across the considerable distance separating them. During the night, the crews of the four ships signaled one another frequently with lanterns. Because of high waves, the lights of one vessel could be seen only intermittently by voyagers aboard another. On the twenty-first night a heavy mist spread over the sea, and the crew of the third ship dropped anchor in an attempt to keep the ship on course. After that night the other two vessels could no longer be sighted. And from then on all voyagers received daily only three cups of water and a cup of dried rice.

On the thirtieth day the sea turned a deep indigo, and towering waves, the consistency of oil, moved slowly across the water, sending the vessel toward mountainous crests, then

*The Vinaya Sect emphasized *vinaya,* or formal monastic discipline. It is known as the Lü Sect in China and as the Ritsu Sect in Japan.

down into hollows. Headwinds were encountered more
frequently once the ship entered these waters. Only the crew
knew the direction in which the ship was traveling. Whenever the wind turned against them, they dropped anchor to
hold their course, and for a whole day, sometimes two,
awaited the return of favorable winds.

On the fortieth day a great storm struck. Although several
storms had already been encountered, the voyagers had never
known such turbulence. The fury struck at noon and did not
abate until noon the following day. For a time seawater
poured into the ship. During the night of the storm, Fushō
heard Kaiyū speaking from pitch darkness over the din of
wind and waves. It was not clear for whom his remarks were
intended, but Fushō sensed that they were directed toward
him.

"What are you thinking about now?" he heard Kaiyū say.

"Nothing in particular," Fushō answered as before.

True, he was terrified by the thought of the ship foundering. Yet Kaiyū's question raised a fury of resentment in him.
Even though it was dark, he readily envisioned Kaiyū's
hulking frame and his brazen glance turned toward him.

"Are you sure?" Kaiyū paused before continuing. "I've
been thinking . . . I don't want to die. I want no part of a
senseless death, and I doubt whether you do either. Well I
don't. No thank you! And another thing. Here we are, shar-
ing the same fate. Yet because we're human beings we're
concerned only with ourselves. Isn't that so?"

He spoke on, but his words were obliterated by the roar of
the wind and sea. Moments later when the din suddenly
subsided, Yōei, who had been waiting for the right moment,
broke the brief lull.

"I've been thinking, too. I've been thinking about the
many Japanese before us who went through the same thing.
Hundreds, maybe thousands, have gone down to the bottom
of the sea. They probably outnumber those who got back
safely to Japan. This is the way religion and learning begin to
develop in any age, in any country—as a result of many lives
sacrificed. If we're lucky and come through this alive, I suppose the least we must do is study hard."

Clearly these words were meant for Kaiyū, and Kaiyū

shouted back at him. No one spoke after that. Argument was impossible during the storm, which prevailed until dawn.

Immediately after Yōei had spoken, Fushō looked around in the darkness for Genrō, who, for some time now, must have been struggling with the terror welling within him. Crouching, unable to utter a word, Genrō impressed Fushō as the most candid and honest of the lot. Kaiyū and Yōei had spoken truths, but Genrō had discarded all pretenses. Although earlier Fushō had been contemptuous of Genrō's undignified timidity, he now found him the most admirable.

Fushō's anxiety differed from that of his three companions. His effort to discipline himself was a continual trial, and he considered his present predicament merely another instance of suffering. For years he had struggled daily against the relentless demands of the flesh. Now fear of death had become his principal anguish. That was all.

Once the storm had passed, everyone spent the days offering prayers to Buddhist and Shinto deities. Prayers were offered to the *kami* of Sumiyoshi Shrine and to the merciful bodhisattva Kannon. Yōei preached the *Lotus Sutra* to his fellow passengers. Kaiyū continued to loll about, but Fushō and Genrō sat up and listened to Yōei. Fushō noticed errors in interpretation from time to time, but he said nothing.

Just off the continent the third ship, waiting for favorable winds, wasted precious days anchored at islands near the coast. Finally it reached the shore of Su-chou. It was already August. The voyagers had been at sea for more than three months since leaving the port of Otsu. The other three vessels also reached the coast of Su-chou during the month of August.

3

The arrival of the ambassador from the court of Japan was reported promptly to the central government by Ch'ien Wei-cheng, Magistrate of Su-chou. Not long after, the officer-interpreter Wei Ching-hsien came to Su-chou to greet the members of the mission and to serve as their host. The Japanese learned that those who received permission to travel on to the capital would sail up the Grand Canal to Pien-chou and from there journey overland to Lo-yang.

19 The Roof Tile of Tempyō

In April of 734—the sixth year of Tempyō in Japan or, in China, the twenty-second year of the era of K'ai-yüan, "Founding of State," during the reign of Emperor Hsüan-tsung*—Ambassador Hironari and his party arrived in Lo-yang. More than seven months had passed since they touched land at Su-chou. They were brought to Lo-yang, the eastern capital, rather than the western capital Ch'ang-an, for Emperor Hsüan-tsung had moved his court earlier in the year.

Hironari and the others must have been disappointed to find the court of the T'ang Emperor in Lo-yang. All previous Japanese missions had been welcomed aboard a government vessel and taken directly to the greater city of Ch'ang-an. Upon arriving at Ch'ang-lo Station, just outside the capital, they were greated by the Imperial Secretary and accorded the first of the formal receptions. They would then proceed on horseback into Ch'ang-an. With hardly a moment given to recovering from the ordeals of travel, they would be summoned from the Ssu-fang House, their lodging during their sojourn, to the I-hua Palace for a ceremonial meeting with the Emperor. Then on to the Lin-te Palace for an informal audience, after which they would be regaled at a reception in the Inner Palace and a lavish banquet in the Hall of the Secretariat. Hironari and others had heard the many splendid ceremonies described time and again. Similar events took place in Lo-yang, of course, but the Japanese emissaries unquestionably wished to occupy center stage in renowned Ch'ang-an and to savor fully the season of spring at the great court of T'ang.

In Lo-yang, Hironari presented the T'ang sovereign with gifts, which included five hundred large pieces of silver, two hundred bolts each of glossed white silk and pongee woven in Mino Province, three hundred bolts each of coarse-textured and fine-textured pongee, five hundred skeins of yellow silk thread, one thousand pounds of fine raw cotton, two hundred bolts of dyed silk, two hundred cotton pads, thirty half-bolts of linen, one hundred half-bolts of linen from Mōda in eastern Japan, one hundred pairs of cotton panels, ten pieces of flint and ten metal strikers, twenty-four gallons

*Hsüan-tsung is the emperor's posthumous title; during his lifetime he was called Ming-huang, or "The Luminous Emperor."

each of camellia oil and sweet-ivy juice, and sixteen gallons
of gold lacquer.

Members of the embassy spent their days eventfully at the
Ssu-fang House, while the students and monks, now wards of
the T'ang government, were being assigned to centers for
learning most appropriate to their individual purpose and
preference. Fushō, Yōei, Kaiyū, and Genrō were all assigned
to the Great Fu-hsien Monastery because Fushō had specified
it in his request. He knew that the eminent monk Ting-p'in,
author of the commentary to Fa Li's *Annotation of the Vinaya
Canon*, had taken up residence there, and he hoped to have
him as his teacher. In such matters Fushō was far more
knowledgeable than his three companions.

The Great Fu-hsien Monastery stood on the site of the
former residence of the Lady Yang, mother of Empress Wu.*
The Ta-yüan-ssu, erected on this site in 675, had subsequently
been renamed Wei-kuo-ssu and, in 691, renamed Great Fu-
hsien-ssu. The grounds of the monastery were spacious, the
pagodas and halls imposing, and accommodations for the
resident monks numerous. The San-chieh Cloister housed a
painting—a depiction of the Buddhist hell—by the celebrated
Wu Tao-hsüan. Wu's paintings were also displayed in the
twin structures supporting the main gate. The Japanese monks
soon learned that the monastery also boasted an illustrious
history as a center for translation. There, they were told, the
late I-ching had translated the *Suvarṇaprabhāsa Sūtra* and other
fundamental scriptures of Buddhism; there, also, the venerable Śubhākarasiṁha a decade before had translated the
Mahāvairocana Sūtra into Chinese.† The young Buddhists
listened with renewed awe.

The Japanese monks enjoyed a relatively carefree existence,
spending most of their time learning to speak Chinese. Only
Kaiyū among them could speak Chinese; where he had
acquired the ability remained a mystery. Lo-yang dazzled
them all. It was much larger than Nara, the capital of Japan,

---

*The empress who ruled China with an iron hand during the latter half
of the seventh century.

†I-ching (635–713), a Chinese monk, studied in India and returned with
many Buddhist texts previously unknown in China. Śubhākarasiṁha
(637–735) came to China from India in 716, and was instrumental in the
propagation of Esoteric Buddhism.

which lacked grandeur by comparison. Lo-yang had, after all, been a royal city as long ago as the Chou Period* and, since then, had been the capital of the Later Han, Northern Wei, and Sui dynasties. Greatness born of history could not be attached to anything in Japan.

The four were given individual rooms, in separate buildings. On leaving Japan, each had been given forty bolts of pongee silk, one hundred pounds of cotton, and eighty half-bolts of linen. Having been made wards of the T'ang government, however, they had no immediate need to barter away their possessions. Once they had settled into the routine at the Great Fu-hsien Monastery, Fushō, Yōei, and Genrō often spent their leisure visiting famed sites and Buddhist edifices in the capital. Everything they beheld was a source of astonishment and wonder. By contrast, Nara, in fact the country known as Japan, seemed pitifully insignificant. Kaiyū visited the same places in Lo-yang, but alone, never in the company of the others.

At the onset of summer, Fushō chanced to meet Kaiyū in front of the latter's quarters and, to his surprise, was invited into his room. Kaiyū, in his characteristically blunt and condescending manner, asked Fushō to describe what had most impressed him since his arrival in China. "There, he's off again," Fushō thought. Though he was tempted to shrug him off as he had during the voyage, he gave a straightforward answer.

"I'm glad I came. If I hadn't, I would never have understood this country we call T'ang."

His reply merely elicited an expression of belittlement from Kaiyū, who countered, "Starving people—that's what I first noticed when we got to China. You must have seen them too. Ever since we landed at Su-chou, every day I've seen hordes of starving people. I've seen more than I can stand."

This was true. The year before their arrival in China, a pre-summer drought and then torrential rains in autumn had left the fields barren, and now there were starving people everywhere. The monks had been told that the famine was the worst in decades.

*The eleventh to the third century, B.C.

"If there were as many distressed people in Japan, there would be chaos. But here in China, the flow of the afflicted is no different from the flow of clouds or the flow of the Yellow River. Why, it's looked upon more or less as a natural phenomenon. I've seen these bonzes from Japan spending all their time grappling with the meaning of single words in the Buddhist scriptures, and they've begun to look like fools to me. The teaching of the Buddha must have a much broader meaning than that. I think the Buddha's teaching is related in some way to the flow of the Yellow River, and of the clouds, and of the afflicted people."

Having said this much with fervor, Kaiyū continued in a calmer vein. "One of these days, when I've adapted to the ways of living in China, I intend to travel about this vast land until my legs give way. I'll be dressed in a Buddhist robe, and I'll beg alms. I'll keep traveling as long as I can keep walking."

Fushō studied the man's large face, and thought that Kaiyū might very well embark on such a venture. "But wouldn't you have to learn something in the process?"

Kaiyū's reply was quick. "Staying glued to a desk! Do you think that's the only way to learn?"

Fushō no longer took offense at Kaiyū as he had done during the voyage. He was aware that Kaiyū possessed some indefinable, unique quality that he himself lacked.

"What on earth made you come to China? What do you intend to do here?" Kaiyū asked.

Fushō answered that he intended to master the *Vinaya* texts; furthermore, having been entrusted with the task of bringing an eminent teacher of monastic rituals back to Japan, he would work toward this end as he pursued his studies.

"It shouldn't be all that difficult to find a Buddhist teacher," Kaiyū said brusquely. "Why make a big thing of it? Why not simply ask someone to go to Japan? What about Tao-hsüan?"

"I suppose you really couldn't expect anyone of stature to go to Japan," Kaiyū continued thoughtfully. "In the first place, most Buddhists who are considered eminent are in their eighties or nineties. You couldn't possibly expect anyone so decrepit to take to a ship. He'd be dead in three days.

You could work at this for years, but it would be the same. Why not get Tao-hsüan to go?"

Fushō was familiar with the name of Tao-hsüan and had seen the monk a few times at a distance. Tao-hsüan, in his mid-thirties, was said to be well versed in the doctrine of the Vinaya Sect and to have studied the T'ien-t'ai and Hua-yen doctrines;* he was known as well for his strict observance of the "Codes of Pure Conduct" in the *Avataṃsaka Sūtra*. He was held in exceptionally high esteem by many Buddhists.

Kaiyū seemed to be telling Fushō that he ought to be satisfied with a lesser man. Yet there was no assurance that even Tao-hsüan would consent to going to Japan, and Fushō expressed his concern.

"You simply have to try him if you want to find out. I've had a few talks with Tao-hsüan. Let me see what I can do. He's bound to say yes. After all, it'll be for the sake of Buddhism."

Fushō attached little importance to what Kaiyū had told him. His suggestions offered no greater promise than that of grasping air. He considered Kaiyū's earlier comment—about the flow of afflicted people—much more in character for him; it revealed a glimmer of that unique quality of character which Fushō had begun to associate with him.

When Yōei and Genrō visited him several days later, Fushō emulated Kaiyū by asking the two monks to relate their most striking impressions of China. Yōei drew himself erect and spoke with animation.

"This country is at the height of its development. This is what has impressed me the most. It's as if flowers that burst into bloom had an awareness of being at their peak. Learning, government, the arts—everything is at its zenith, surely to be followed by decline. We ought to take whatever can be got out of this empire, and do it now. Students from foreign lands have been attracted to the twin capitals like bees to nectar. They're swarming about the flowers as we are, sucking in the nectar."

"This is off the subject," he added, "but I see this vast population eating, sleeping, and staying alive, sustained by the instincts of living creatures, wholly unconcerned with

*Known in Japan as Tendai and Kegon.

Buddhist thought, or with government, or with learning."

Kaiyū had referred to "the flow of clouds and of the Yellow River," and Yōei to "the instincts of living creatures." As Fushō started to remark that the two had expressed much the same thing, Yōei broke in.

"Kaiyū! What does he know? What can he do besides startle people with his odd prattle? If he has any talent at all, it's his ability to speak Chinese. Even so, there's no telling how well he speaks it." Yōei scowled whenever the conversation turned to Kaiyū. He was detested by Kaiyū, whom he treated with equal disdain.

Fushō then prodded Genrō for a response.

"I've become aware that I want to go back to Japan," Genrō said in a plaintive tone suggesting regret. "I've become aware that Japan is the best place to be. If one is Japanese, one simply cannot, for all the world, live a meaningful life anywhere but in Japan. Whatever anyone else says won't change this." He added that he might be willing, should it be possible, to go back with the ambassadorial mission when it left for Japan in November.

Genrō had not seemed despondent during the spring when they first came to Lo-yang. But with the advent of summer, homesickness, which had assailed him during the voyage, possessed him again. He was listless and melancholy. Fushō once more thought that Genrō's complaints rang truer than the words of either Kaiyū or Yōei. Genrō had, in fact, called Fushō's attention to his own nostalgia for Japan, less than a half-year after arriving in China.

Fushō spoke of Tao-hsüan and the earlier discussion with Kaiyū.

"I know of him," Yōei said. "I've heard that Tao-hsüan is an upright man, that he's outstanding among the younger monks. We'd be lucky if he would decide to go, but I doubt that he would consent without giving the matter considerable thought. Furthermore, a proposal of this nature mustn't be presented too hastily." Yōei, like Fushō, attached little importance to what Kaiyū had said.

Four days later, however, Kaiyū came to see Fushō again. He strode into the room and spoke without bothering to sit down.

"He said he'll go. I've taken care of the first stage, and the rest is up to you. If you're at all serious, you ought to talk to him. Here, I've prepared some information on him."

He handed a slip of paper to Fushō and hurried away. Noted down in Kaiyū's calligraphy, distinctive for its unconventional flourishes, were these facts: "Tao-hsüan, a native of Hsü-chou, age thirty-four, lay surname Wei, a descendant of Lord Ling of the Kingdom of Wei of the Spring and Autumn Era, a student of Hsin-suan of the Great Fu-hsien Monastery and of Fu-chih of Hua-yen Temple."

4

The party of the Japanese ambassador to the T'ang court was to return home in two months, in November. Fushō and the others had many opportunities to meet with Japanese who had preceded them and had now completed their studies, and were preparing to sail back to Japan.

First they met Gembō, of whom they had known when they were in Japan. Gembō had studied the Yuishiki doctrine under Gien at Ryūmon-ji in Japan and received recognition as one of Gien's "seven superior disciples."* He had come to China in 716, nineteen years before. He had also studied the Fa-hsiang doctrine under the tutelage of Chih-chou of Pu-yang and won the admiration of Emperor Hsüan-tsung, who granted him the third court rank and bestowed upon him the purple robe of state in recognition of his scholarly attainments. When Gembō came to the Great Fu-hsien Monastery in the company of two Chinese monks—for a fond last look at the famed monastery of Lo-yang—the four student monks from Japan greeted him with humility, for they acknowledged his preëminence among those who had preceded them to China. Gembō now around fifty, was a stocky man with thick distinctive brows, and was the only Japanese monk to have been awarded the purple robe. Fushō watched in awe.

Gembō evidently was in a hurry and appeared ill at ease. He asked each of them about their studies, offered a few

*Also among the "seven" were Ryūson, as well as Gyōgi and Rōben, who come into the story in Chapter XVI. In Japan, the Yuishiki (Chinese: Wei-shih) doctrine was quickly absorbed into the teachings of the Hossō (Chinese: Fa-hsiang) Sect of Buddhism.

words of encouragement, then made a quick round of the monastery grounds, and was gone. They felt as if a strong gust of wind had swept by them. Fushō had hoped that Gembō would advise them about the pitfalls of studying in a foreign country, or tell them how they might best profit from their studies. He did, after all, share the blood of their race; prominent though he may have become, he had arrived to China as they had, a Buddhist monk in quest of knowledge. But Fushō was not given an opportunity to speak.

The four monks sat and talked about the man who had appeared before them fleetingly and in whose footsteps they would follow. It had been some time since the four had sat together. Their faces glowed with excitement. Fushō easily visualized Gembō back in a monastery in Nara, seated before an overflowing audience of Japanese monks, lecturing on the principles of the Fa-hsiang doctrine. Yet he was disturbed by some details of his image, the dark brows, for instance, that called to mind the face of a warrior, the impassive steadiness of Gembō's gaze, the aloofness that permitted no cordiality whatever, and the abruptness, unbecoming a teacher of distinction. When Fushō mentioned them, Yōei defended those very qualities as marks of his greatness. Gembō was able to attain prominence as a scholar in the T'ang empire, Yōei insisted, precisely because it was not his nature to extend fraternal solicitude toward every countryman he chanced to meet.

Genrō excitedly disclosed fragments of information he had gathered: Gembō would take back five thousand scrolls of sutras and commentaries, for instance. Kaiyū listened quietly and was the last to speak.

"Both Gembō and Gyōgi were disciples of Gien. They're probably about the same age. Gembō came to China in order to study at the Pu-yang Monastery, but Gyōgi remained in Japan and worked among the common folk. While Gembō concentrated on doctrine, Gyōgi dispensed medicine to the sick and recited prayers on behalf of those who suffered. He built new bridges and preached on the streets. Gembō studied in a foreign land and mastered the Hossō doctrine. He proved himself a better scholar than others, and was awarded a purple robe by the sovereign of the empire. Gyōgi took his place at the head of a horde of beggars, the sick, and the distressed, and he walked from town to village, constantly preaching."

Kaiyū cut himself off as he realized that he had reached an extreme pitch of excitement. The sharpness of his tone had silenced the others. He laughed to shield his embarrassment.

"So it seems. Really, I wouldn't know who is the greater of the two." Abruptly he turned his back on the others and sauntered off.

A few days later, Fushō met with Kibi Makibi in a room in the Ssu-fang House, where the ambassador's party was lodged. Makibi had come to China with Abé Nakamaro as a member of the eighth ambassadorial mission in 717, a year after Gembō's arrival. Besides specializing in the Chinese classics, Makibi had studied divination, calendric mathematics, and astronomy, and his reputation as a scholar rivaled that of Gembō.

Small in stature, Makibi seemed to Fushō to be a rather mild and ordinary man. Had one persisted in finding some idiosyncracy that would set him apart from the ordinary, one might have noticed that Makibi had lived so long in China that he gave the impression of being Chinese. His complexion was Chinese; his eyes, too, were unmistakably the placid eyes of a Chinese. He had come to China at the age of twenty-three. He was now forty.

At the moment, Makibi was presenting the ambassador's party with the list of goods he would be taking back with him, and was in the process of negotiating with the official in charge of packing and shipment. He was calling out items for the official to note down, then peering unhurriedly at the sheet to make certain each one had been listed correctly. He seemed oblivious to Fushō's presence in the room.

Makibi was taking back an infinite variety of goods. Fushō could not possibly have estimated the bulk. The *T'ang Rites* in one hundred and thirty volumes, I-hsing's *Great Calendar*,*

*The Great Calendar, instituted in T'ang China in 729 and used until 762, was adopted in Japan in 763 and used for about a century. A year in this calendar was approximately the equivalent of a solar year.

the twelve-volume compendium of studies of the *Great Calendar*, the ten-volume *Essentials of Writings on Music*, a bronze tuning pipe, an iron sun-dial rule, twenty armor-piercing arrows, ten flat-trajectory arrows, a variety of horn bows—the list went on and on.

For a time it was rumored that Abé Nakamaro might also return to Japan, although he was now an officer of the T'ang government. As Councilor of the Left, he was charged with an advisory function in addition to such duties as attending on the emperor's person, accompanying the emperor in processions, and keeping the royal steeds and carriages in readiness. His official tasks should have brought him to Lo-yang, but Fushō and his companions had yet to meet this student, whose career had brought him unique fame.

Fushō learned that another monk-scholar from Japan was now in residence at the Great Fu-hsien Monastery. When he mentioned this to Genrō, Genrō immediately set about finding the following information: The monk was named Keiun; he had come to China by himself thirty years before and had been studying the San-lun and Fa-hsiang doctrines; he would be returning to Japan aboard one of the Japanese ships.

"Shall we go and meet him?" Genrō asked, eager, as always, to meet with another Japanese.

Fushō agreed that learning about the experiences of any man who had spent thirty years in the T'ang empire would be worthwhile.

Keiun was spending the days prior to sailing in the seclusion of a small room at the monastery. A faint smile played on his gentle face as he received the two visitors and invited them to sit on chairs placed in a corner. Though his hair was speckled with gray and his general appearance suggested he might be nearing sixty, his complexion was hardly that of an old man. He told them his health was impaired, but he showed no signs of debility. And his face bore no creases to betray the arduous strains of serious study.

"Although I've spent thirty years in China, I never found anything that really interested me. I daresay it would have made little difference had I stayed in Japan. Who knows? I might have been better off had I spent those years living in the countryside of Japan."

Keiun spoke softly, and with no apparent intent to disparage himself. Although he had been told that Keiun came to China to study Buddhist doctrines, Fushō sensed that he was trying to steer the conversation away from the subject. He emboldened himself to ask a question.

"And what will you take back to Japan?"

"Only myself," the monk answered. Evidently he was concerned only with having his age-worn body transported from China back to Japan.

"I doubt whether any other Japanese has spent as many years as you have in China."

"There couldn't be many. Those who did without exception made something of themselves before returning to Japan. I might be the only one who didn't amount to anything . . . " His remarks trailed off as he sought to recollect. "Oh, yes. There's one other man. There's Gōgyō. He's been in China close to thirty years."

"What kind of person is he?"

"Like myself, a monk of the Hossō sect. I urged him to go back to Japan with me, but he didn't seem anxious to return. He's another who didn't get out into the sunlight." Keiun looked pensive when he said this; neither Fushō nor Genrō could comprehend the meaning of his remark.

The two students soon took their leave of Keiun. Once outside his room, they were struck by what seemed a dismal truth. True, Keiun had come to China of his own free will. He had not been sent by the Japanese government, and so he had been free to decide how he would spend his time there. Keiun, who wore the clerical robe and yet did not aspire to taking so much as a single scroll of the scriptures back to Japan, appeared a pitiful and foolish man indeed in the eyes of the young monks.

In the evening a few days later, Genrō came to see Fushō.

"I've been to see him. This man is quite different. Really, you ought to meet him."

Genrō had been to see Gōgyō. He was an oddity, but in what respect Genrō could not readily explain. Fushō would have to meet him and see for himself. A few days afterward, Fushō heard more about Gōgyō, this time from Yōei.

"Though he's spent more than twenty years in this country, all he knows about China are a few monasteries. He's been traveling from one monastery to another, making copies of Buddhist texts. He seems to have seen nothing and met no one, but apparently he's transcribed an amazing number of writings."

"What is he like?" Fushō asked.

"I couldn't tell you. He may be a man of greatness, and yet he could be a fool."

These reports aroused Fushō's curiosity. He was inclined to visit the curious monk, thoughts of whom persisted inexplicably in his mind. However, with the coming of autumn he resumed his studies and, as had been his custom in Japan, begrudged himself even a moment away from his desk. He would soon finish the twelve scrolls of the *Manual of Vinaya Sect Rituals*, which he had failed to do during the voyage. Then he would begin reading Fa Li's *Annotation of the Vinaya Canon*, unfamiliar to him until he came to China. Although every minute seemed precious, he was reminded of the possibility of Gōgyō's leaving on the forthcoming sailing and decided finally to meet with him. Early one afternoon he went out to a nameless little temple on the outskirts of the city.

He found Gōgyō in a small northerly room, seated at his desk, with a writing brush in hand. Although Fushō at first felt as if he had come into a dank, cheerless cell, when he sat down opposite Gōgyō and looked about the room, he found nothing exceptional. It was somewhat dimmer than those on the opposite side of the building. Strewn about the room lay a number of bundles of inscribed sheets, probably Buddhist sutras or other kinds of ancient documents. Gōgyō sat amidst the clutter, quite as if he had been sitting thus a very long time. He looked up at his visitor. He may have been close to fifty; but it was difficult to guess his age, for his frail, diminutive body was the body of a boy that had somehow taken on age. He cut a dismal, most unimpressive figure.

"Are you a friend of that fellow—what was his name?— who called on me the other day?" He spoke haltingly. Although it was only the beginning of autumn and too early for the cold to be felt, Gōgyō sat trembling, his hands tucked under his thighs.

"Will you be returning on this sailing?" Fushō asked him.
"Well . . . I . . . " The vague beginning came in a low
murmur. Fushō expected him to continue, but Gōgyō said
no more. In an effort to encourage conversation, Fushō mentioned the names of several men who would be returning to
Japan; with each name Gōgyō lifted his gaze, but said nothing. If anything, his face showed a trace of embarrassment.

"Have you ever met him?" Fushō would repeat the same
question as he cited a name, but invariably he received the
same response, "Well . . . I . . . " Evidently Gōgyō had
not met any of them. Perhaps he had not had the opportunity
to meet Nakamaro or Gembō or Makibi, but how could it
be that he had never heard of them? Because Gōgyō's expression betrayed embarrassment at the mere mention of a Japanese name, Fushō began to suspect that the monk felt
humiliated because of his own lack of achievement. However, this was not the case. Gōgyō was discomfited, Fushō
realized finally, because he was at a loss to respond to queries
concerning matters in which he had no interest.

Of the many Japanese faces Fushō had seen since his arrival
in China, Gōgyō's had been affected the least by living in
China. His body, small and spare, was like that of a peasant
anywhere in Japan. Because Gōgyō said nothing except in
answer to questions, Fushō began to feel as if he were harry-
ing him.

"You've been in Ch'ang-an, haven't you?"
"I have."
"How many years did you spend there?"
"Well, let me see . . . five years? No, that's not right. I've
been there a number of times . . . well, perhaps seven or
eight years altogether."
"When did you come to Lo-yang?"
"I came here last year." Then he added, "I've been here
many times, of course, and so I've spent all of four years
here . . . maybe five."
"What have you been doing?"
"You see it here." Gōgyō inclined his chin toward his desk.
"I've still much to do. I simply started too late. You see,
I made the mistake of wasting a few years trying to study.
I wasn't aware of my limitations, and I realized much too

late that no amount of study would do me much good. What I think Japan needs most right now are faithful copies of Buddhist sutras and commentaries, but those copies have got to be accurate to the word. Texts being sent over to Japan these days are hardly reliable."

Only in this instance did Gōgyō express anything approximating an opinion of his own, and this he spoke rapidly, quivering all the while. His quivering was a nervous movement.

5

In mid-September, Tajihi Hironari and members of the ninth embassy to the court of China departed from the capital city of Lo-yang to begin their journey homeward. The month of October was drawing to a close when they embarked on four ships at the port of Su-chou.

Aboard the lead vessel, in the company of Ambassador Hironari, were Kibi Makibi and the monk Gembō, who had received early assurances of returning to Japan. Rumors of Nakamaro's impending departure for Japan were eventually silenced. He was an officer of the T'ang government and a favorite of Emperor Hsüan-tsung. He was not free, therefore, to dictate his own course of action. Although Nakamaro had petitioned the emperor that he might return to Japan and be reunited with his aged parents, his request had been denied.

I crave to be righteous, but hollow fame is my reward.
Faithful to my sovereign, yet unfilial to my parents,
Am I to languish unavailingly in their debt?
When will be the year of my return?

This verse by Nakamaro, contained in *The Contents of the Anthology of Japanese Poetry, Ancient and Modern,** expresses the yearning he felt at the time.

A variety of voyagers boarded the second ship, which was under the command of the vice-ambassador, Nakatomi Nashiro. Besides Tao-hsüan, whom Fushō and Yōei had persuaded to go to Japan, the varied group included the learned Chinese monk Li-chiang, the Brahman monk, Bodhisenna,

*An eleventh-century study of the *Kokinshū*, the first imperial anthology of Japanese poetry, compiled in 905.

the Annamese monk Fo-t'ieh, two Chinese named Huang-fu Tung-chao and Yüan Fu-ch'ing, and the Persian, Li-mi-i. The eldest among these exotic passengers was the Indian monk Bodhisenna; he was then thirty-eight. The youngest was the seventeen-year-old Yüan Fu-ch'ing, who later was to become a Japanese subject and a famous performer of Chinese music. Keiun, whose many years in the T'ang empire had borne no fruit, was aboard ship three, commanded by the praetor Heguri Hironari.

The four ships set sail together from Su-chou, and the first news concerning the voyagers reached the young student-monks in China during the New Year season of 735, on the night of the Lantern Festival, the fifteenth of January. Entrances of Chinese houses in both the city and the countryside were adorned with lanterns for several nights before and after the fifteenth, to celebrate the eve of spring; and merrymaking in the streets lasted until dawn. Nightly during the festival, the streets of Lo-yang became streams of lantern light. Some houses were decorated with a great many lanterns suspended from the eaves; others displayed multiple rows of lanterns suspended from tiered racks of fantastic size or mounted on huge shelves. Street corners were lighted by bonfires, and people strolled, sang, and danced in the light of flames that turned night into day.

On the night of the festival, Fushō waited for Yōei and Genrō in his room. The three monks had planned to stroll and view the festivities till the late hours of the night. Genrō came at eight o'clock, and the two waited almost an hour for Yōei. When he came he brought news of the four ships that had set sail from Su-chou in October. They had encountered a storm almost immediately; one vessel had returned to the coast of Yüeh-chou (present-day Chekiang Province) and then set sail again for Japan.

"No one seems to know which of the four ships touched at Yüeh-chou," Yōei said. "The one that did might be the only one with a chance of getting back to Japan. According to the crew, the other ships may not have survived the storm."

Yōei had just been given the news by monks from Yang-chou. His face was shrouded in gloom as he related it; so, too, were the faces of his companions as they listened.

With heavy hearts the Japanese monks went out into the festive streets of the alien city. The gate to the Yen-fu Quarter was kept open that night, although normally it would be closed at an early hour. They crossed the canal and walked along the embankment through the Yung-t'ai Quarter. As they neared the South City, they could see the night sky aflame with crimson. Soon they were in bright, crowded streets where people were dancing with abandon. Fushō had browsed through several books in order to learn something about the festivities that took place during the celebration referred to popularly as "the stringing of lanterns on the eve of spring," or "the viewing of lantern lights during the first full moon." As he threaded his way through the crowd, he recalled a line from a verse composed by Emperor Yang-ti of the Sui dynasty: "Lantern-lit trees give off a thousand lights; flowering flames infuse the branches with life"—a description befitting the festive luminescence before him. But the lyrical words and the suggestion of gaiety were quickly transmuted, in Fushō's mind, to forlorn emptiness.

The three monks slipped out of the South City, where for an hour they had watched the merriment, and into a quieter, dimmer area in the vicinity of the Chi-chuan Quarter. They talked little as they walked. Once the brightness of the city was behind them, however, Yōei began to think out loud: they ought to be thankful should even one of the ships reach Japan; barring some remarkable, divine intervention, there was little hope of all four vessels reaching Japanese shores.

"I wonder if it wouldn't be for the best," he added, "if the lead ship were the one to arrive safely? Gembō and Makibi are on it. Or should we place our hopes on the second ship, which is carrying Tao-hsüan?"

Yōei had placed Gembō and Makibi on one end of a balancing scale and Tao-hsüan on the other, and was comparing the benefits to be derived from their presence in Japan. Fushō could not think in these terms, and so he said nothing.

Genrō expressed what apparently had been preying on his mind. Timidly he confessed the following: had it been at all possible, he would have set sail for Japan with the ambassador's party; he had been sorely tempted to plead ill health and request passage home; had he sailed with them, however, he might have lost his life.

"It's the same with us," Genrō went on. "There's no assurance of our getting back to Japan safely. We might get back to Japan, and yet we might not. For all we know, we might be accumulating knowledge only to take it down with us to the bottom of the sea."

Fushō saw an almost feminine frailty in Genrō, a man who looked ahead with such trepidation to a voyage in the distant future. Yōei had made the same observation. "Why can't the three of us sail separately?" he asked. "Then we'll only have to worry about one ship getting back safely." His sarcasm pressed the others into silence.

The monks had returned to the bright avenue leading to the Ch'ang-hsia Gate. There in the milling throng they were quickly engulfed by shrieks and shouts and the metallic cacophony of orchestral instruments. Bonfires occasionally gave off bursts of sparks. Yōei, his body erect, strode with firm steps through the crowd, his face appearing pale in the light of the bonfires. Genrō fell behind as he drifted with the throng that pressed against him from all sides. His face was flushed. Fushō's cold eyes glinted occasionally as he looked up at the crimson night sky. Not that he was unconcerned about the fate of Gembō or Makibi or Tao-hsüan, but the image which persisted in his thoughts was that of the aged Keiun—the monk who had spent half a lifetime in China, had accomplished nothing, and was taking back to Japan naught save his physical self.

A month went by, and in mid-February more news of the Japanese ships was received in Lo-yang. The vessel that had drifted back to the coast of Yüeh-chou was Ambassador Hironari's lead ship; it had again set sail and had reached Tané Island* on the twentieth of November.

It was rumored around that time that the ship carrying the vice-ambassador Nashiro had reached the shores of Nanhai† with no loss in lives. Shortly thereafter, the rumor was con-

---

*An island eighteen miles off the southern coast of Kyushu.
†The area of present-day Canton, more than a thousand miles south of the port of embarkation.

firmed by the reappearance of Nashiro and several others in
Lo-yang. Fushō and Yōei met with Nashiro and offered consoling words. They were told that Tao-hsüan and the rest had
remained at the port in Su-chou, awaiting another sailing.

In the intercalary month of November, when the bite of
the wintry cold was first beginning to be felt, Nashiro left
Lo-yang in order to embark again on his journey homeward.
Emperor Hsüan-tsung on that occasion entrusted Nashiro
with an "Imperial Missive to the King of the Japanese Nation," a document drafted by the minister Chang Chiu-ling.*

Just before Nashiro left Lo-yang, a report describing the
fate of the third ship was received from the magistrate of
Kuang-chou in south China. The vessel had drifted far south-
ward to Champa;† most of the voyagers had been killed by
the Cham natives. The praetor Heguri Hironari and three
others were the only survivors. Emperor Hsüan-tsung
promptly ordered the territorial governor of Annam to hasten to rescue the four survivors. When Fushō and Genrō heard
this news, they talked about Keiun. Neither could believe
that the aged monk would be among the four survivors.

In the spring of the following year, 736, there were two
significant turns of events in the lives of the Japanese student-
monks, then in their third year of residence in China. The
first was an achievement: Yōei, Fushō, Genrō, and Kaiyū
had taken the Supreme Clerical Vow, administered to them
by Ting-p'in of the Great Fu-hsien Monastery. The other was
Kaiyū's disappearance shortly after they had taken the vow.

Kaiyū did not maintain close ties with the three other Japanese even though they all resided at the Great Fu-hsien-
ssu. Only with Fushō did he enjoy an easy friendship. Every
so often, one of them would think of the other and visit him.

Whenever Kaiyū came for a visit, he found Fushō at his
desk studying. If Fushō went to see Kaiyū, however, Kaiyū
had visitors in his room. And his visitors were a varied lot.
Besides Chinese, Fushō occasionally saw Brahmans, as well
as monks from Champa and Silla. Kaiyū would always be

---

*Renowned both as a man of letters and as a brilliant minister of state,
Chang fell from power when he attempted to thwart the rise of Li Lin-fu,
who is brought into this story in the next chapter.

†The area of present-day Vietnam; it lay south of Annam, then a pro-
tectorate of the T'ang empire.

chatting jovially, although most likely in pidgin, with the monks who had come from foreign lands.

After the beginning of the new year Kaiyū, who had not visited for some time, came to see Fushō. He told Fushō that he intended to slip away soon from the Great Fu-hsien Monastery and set out on a journey as a mendicant. Fushō was not suprised. He had been expecting Kaiyū some day to carry out what he had once vowed he would. He made no attempt at dissuasion, but instead asked Kaiyū where his travels might take him. Kaiyū replied that he had no particular destination in mind; he would have little choice but to follow the well-worn path that others had passed, to Mount Wu-t'ai and Mount T'ien-lung; from there he would most likely veer off in a different direction in order to visit Mount Lu.* He spoke casually about it, as if it concerned someone else.

"Once I've visited Mount Lu, I'll travel about the vast land of China. I feel certain I'll come across something that will have special meaning."

"What would it be?"

"I'm not certain. But I know there is something extraordinary in this country, and I hope to discover what it is as I roam this vast land. I'll never find out unless I travel." Kaiyū seemed enraptured merely by the thought of roving about the spacious expanse of China.

Fushō could not believe that China, vast though it may be, would contain anything extraordinary. Whatever might be considered extraordinary probably lay hidden in a Buddhist text as yet unknown to him. The flow of new Buddhist texts from India into China was continual. The forest of Buddhist texts, even more than the land of China, was vast and boundless.

Several days later at the Chien-ch'un Gate, Fushō bade farewell to Kaiyū, who was dressed as a mendicant. The waters of the Yi River had taken in the warmth of the sunlight of early spring, and the willows on the banks swayed gently in a mild breeze. Buds of the plum blossom would

---

*All are renowned Buddhist sites. Mounts Wu-t'ai and T'ien-lung are some 300 miles north of Lo-yang and not far south of the Great Wall. Mount Lu, near the Yangtze River, is more than 400 miles south of Lo-yang.

soon be unfolding. Strollers could be seen delighting in the advent of the new season.

Kaiyū's disappearance was viewed with relative indifference, for in those times a great many monks traveled from one monastery to another begging alms. The only consequence of note was Kaiyū's forfeiture of his sustenance by the T'ang government. Luckily the incident attracted little notice, and in due time was consigned to oblivion. Yōei alone denounced what he said was Kaiyū's unpardonable flouting of the responsibilities of a student-monk sent to China for the purpose of study.

During the spring and summer, Fushō made several visits to the monastery in the outlying district in order to see Gōgyō. As always the aging monk was engrossed in the work of transcribing sutras.

During his first visit, Fushō at one point in the conversation remarked on the tragic fate that Keiun might have encountered. Only then did Gōgyō, to whom the task of transcribing sacred texts had become the sole reason for existence, lift his head slightly, and gaze wistfully into the distance. But in an instant his expression reverted to one of total unconcern. He said nothing about Keiun's possibly grievous fate. Gōgyō had never had reason to esteem Keiun, but neither had he seemed to regard him with disdain. Nonetheless, Fushō was both puzzled and astonished by Gōgyō's apparent unconcern.

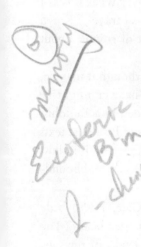

On Gōgyō's desk lay a transcribed copy of a sutra that Fushō had never seen. It was titled *Methods of Seeking Retentive Powers from Ākāśa-garbha*. In truth, Fushō was seldom familiar with the titles of texts Gōgyō was busy transcribing. Gōgyō had accumulated a fantastic number of scrolls. Mostly they were copies of writings that had been translated from Sanskrit into Chinese by I-ching, who had died twenty-four years before, in 715, at the Ta-chien-fu Monastery in Ch'ang-an.

I-ching had been devoted to the *Vinaya*, or monastic, aspect of Buddhism, and had striven, through frequent lectures, to promote the spread of the doctrine. The works he had translated dealt generally with the *Vinaya*. Whenever Fushō needed information about texts pertaining to the *Vinaya*, he went to Gōgyō, who would lend him a copy he had transcribed, or would tell him where he might obtain a copy and describe the contents to him.

Gōgyō was at his desk constantly, making copies of texts I-ching had translated. One had the impression that it was for this purpose he had been given life in this world. On his third visit, Fushō saw Gōgyō with the *Mahāvairocana Sūtra* spread out before him, copying it in a style of calligraphy identical with the original. Gōgyō's calligraphy always resembled that of the text he was transcribing. He took special pains to achieve this resemblance. It seemed that Gōgyō was a man who possessed nothing he might call his own. And yet, this activity may have given him the one modest pleasure he derived from life, work that kept him perennially at his desk, writing brush in hand, oblivious to the passing of time.

The sutra Gōgyō was now transcribing was another with which Fushō was wholly unfamiliar. When Fushō mentioned this, Gōgyō, in his customary halting speech, explained that the text was not a translation made by I-ching. Since spring, Gōgyō said, he had been transcribing scriptures of Esoteric Buddhism, translated into Chinese by Śubhākarasiṁha, who had died the year before at the age of ninety-nine.

"I believe the last time you were here I was transcribing the *Ākāśa-garbha*, something Śubhākarasiṁha translated about twenty years ago, when he was residing at the Bodhi Cloister in Ch'ang-an. What I have here is a work he translated when he was at the Great Fu-hsien-ssu a few years ago, the *Mahā-vairocana Sūtra*, in which all the principles of Esoteric Buddhism are explained. So far as I know, there aren't many copies of these around."

Gōgyō evidently possessed a consummate knowledge. Fushō, for one, would scarcely have known where to begin looking if he had had to locate such sutras. The transcribing of I-ching's translations had become Gōgyō's principal task. Only when he could not obtain I-ching's works would he spend time transcribing other writings.

Fushō visited with Gōgyō only occasionally, but he derived much pleasure from their companionship. The gloominess of Gōgyō's personality, which had struck Fushō when they first met, seemed to vanish gradually as the visits multiplied.

What had not changed, however, was Gōgyō's habitual quivering.

The court of the T'ang Emperor had been situated in Lo-yang, the eastern capital, since the first month of 734. Toward the end of summer, the city became alive with rumors of the Emperor's imminent return to Ch'ang-an, the capital in the west. Shortly thereafter, Fushō, Yōei, and Genrō were given their first opportunity to meet with Abé Nakamaro. A messenger conveyed Nakamaro's wish to have the three monks present for consultation at the Central Ministry.

On the appointed day, the three young monks entered the Left Gate of the Imperial Quarters and proceeded to the government offices. The Central Ministry was situated not far from the Ssu-fang House, where members of the Japanese mission had been lodged. There, in a room of the ministry building, the monks met with the one-time student from Japan, who had won fame as an officer of the T'ang government and a distinguished man of letters. Nakamaro was then thirty-seven years old. He was a stocky man of medium height, with a face that never betrayed inner agitation. As Makibi and Gembō had been expressionless, so also was Nakamaro. He made no special gesture to acknowledge the monks as fellow countrymen and proceeded directly to the business at hand, which he described succinctly: Emperor Hsüan-tsung would be returning to Ch'ang-an, the western capital; if they wished to move to Ch'ang-an, he would arrange for them to be taken westward with the imperial cortege. Yōei and Genrō accepted the offer immediately, but Fushō asked to be given two days in which to make a decision. Because he had been furthering his study of Buddhism under the gracious tutelage of Ting-p'in, he would first have to consult his teacher.

Two days later, Fushō again called on Nakamaro at the Central Ministry. Nakamaro was aloof, as he had been before. When Fushō conveyed his wish to be taken to Ch'ang-an, Nakamaro inclined his head in a gesture of acknowledgment and said he would make the necessary arrangements. But on that occasion, perhaps because Fushō had come alone, Nakamaro inquired briefly about the progress he was making in his studies.

The Emperor's cortege left Lo-yang on the second of October. Thanks to Nakamaro's intercession, the three student-monks from Japan were given permission, through an imperial decree, to accompany the Emperor's procession. They arrived in Ch'ang-an on the twentieth. Emperor Hsüan-tsung, during his return journey, visited Shan-chou in order to praise the administration of the prefect, Lu Huan, and he inscribed a poem of praise on the wall of Lu's office. The act befitted the flamboyant emperor.

In Ch'ang-an, the three monks were assigned quarters in separate monasteries—Yōei at the Ta-an-kuo-ssu, Genrō at Ho-en-ssu, and Fushō at Ch'ung-fu-ssu. The Ta-an-kuo and Ho-en monasteries were not far apart, both being situated to the east of the Imperial Quarter. Ch'ung-fu-ssu, which was to be Fushō's residence, stood on a site west of the Imperial Quarter, some distance away from the monasteries where his two friends resided.

Shortly after Fushō and his companions arrived in the western capital, Heguri Hironari and the three other survivors of the third ship, which had drifted far south to Champa, returned to Ch'ang-an. All four men were changed beyond recognition. They were to spend two successive New Year seasons in Ch'ang-an before resuming their homeward journey. In March of 738 (the tenth year of the Tempyō Era), Abé Nakamaro arranged for their passage, and the four men sailed from Shantung Peninsula to the state of Pohai, and from there they set sail in the company of the Pohai ambassador bound for Japan. The vessel encountered a storm on the way and drifted into the coast of Dewa Province in northern Japan. The men arrived in the capital city of Nara in late autumn of the following year, 739. The lead ship of Ambassador Tajihi Hironari had touched land at Tané Island on the twentieth of November in 734; the ambassadorial sword had been returned to the Emperor in March of 735. Nashiro, the vice-ambassador, had also returned earlier, aboard the second craft, and had presented himself at the court of the Emperor in August of 736. The third ship had taken four-and-a-half years longer than the lead vessel, and three years longer than the second to return to Japan. By the time Nashiro arrived back in Japan in 736, Ambassador

Tajihi Hironari, who had been promoted to the third court grade and appointed middle councilor upon his return, had been dead six months.

The fate of the fourth ship was never known.

6

Ch'ang-an, a major center for Buddhist studies as well as the capital of the great T'ang empire, attracted throngs of men of scholarly and virtuous attainments from within and without the nation. Dharmacandra, who had brought a new religious doctrine into China from eastern India, was in Ch'ang-an. Vajrabodhi, the exalted monk of Esoteric Buddhism and also from India, came to Ch'ang-an in 736, the same year that the Japanese monks arrived, and was in residence at Ta-chien-fu Monastery. It was also in 736 that Wu Tao-hsüan, then residing at Chingkung-ssu, painted another of his famed visions of hell. In 738, the twenty-sixth year of K'ai-yüan, monasteries named K'ai-yüan-ssu were established in the various counties. In 739, the Prajñā Dais was erected in Ch'ang-an.

Fushō devoted his days at the Ch'ung-fu-ssu to fulfilling his initial objective of mastering the *Vinaya* texts. The monastery boasted an illustrious history as a center for sutra translation as well as Buddhist studies; Divākara had produced his translations, Fa-ts'ang had written his "Commentary on the Principles of *Mahāyāna*," Bodhiruci had translated the *Mahāratnakūta Sūtra*, and, more recently, Chih-sheng had compiled the *K'ai-yüan Era Catalogue of Translations of Sutras*—all at Ch'ung-fu-ssu. Moreover, Huai-su, the academic arch-rival of Ting-p'in, at one time had propagated the teachings of the Vinaya Sect at the monastery. Ting-p'in was the monk who had administered the monastic vows to Fushō and his companions. Thus Ch'ung-fu-ssu had meaningful associations for Fushō.

In his studies, Fushō relied heavily on three texts: Fa Li's *Annotation of the Vinaya Canon*, the commentary on Fa Li's work written by Ting-p'in, and Ling Yu's explication of Ting-p'in's commentary. He also explored the dissident doctrine of Huai-su as well as the Nan-shan wing of the Vinaya Sect. Although Yōei tended to regard Fushō's approach to learning as frivolous, Fushō paid him no heed and persisted in his quest for knowledge. Yōei was content just learning Ting-p'in's doctrine, which prevailed at the Ta-an-kuo-ssu.

Genrō was studying the Vinaya aspects of the T'ien-t'ai and Pure Land doctrines of Buddhism. In Ch'ang-an, he was once again engrossed in study, and it seemed in accord with his character to take an interest in the Pure Land, a doctrine as yet unknown in Japan. Yōei and Fushō were at times amazed by Genrō's brilliance of mind; but this brilliance was actually an impediment, for it seemed to deprive him of the patience required to study any one subject in depth.

In the summer of 742—the first year of the new era of T'ien-pao* in China, the fourteenth year of Tempyō in Japan—Yōei and Fushō, who had been in Ch'ang-an more than five years, began thinking of returning to Japan. There were two reasons for this. For one, a Korean monk who had come recently from Japan brought disturbing news concerning Tao-hsüan. Though Tao-hsüan had gone to Japan in 736 for the express purpose of initiating orthodox monasticism, he had been unable to fulfill his mission owing to the lack of qualified monks to assist in the ministration of vows. He was in residence at the Daian-ji, doing nothing more than lecturing on *Vinaya* texts and the *Manual of Vinaya Sect Rituals*.

Yōei and Fushō were quite distressed by the tidings. On reflection, they were reminded that they had already spent six years in Ch'ang-an and that a decade had flown by since their arrival in China. Fushō was approaching the age of forty, and Yōei was already past it.

Yōei held himself accountable for the failure of orthodox monasticism to be observed in Japan and, from that day on, was possessed by his obligation to dispatch teachers of monastic discipline to Japan. Fushō was not unconcerned, but he could not imagine their fulfilling such a task quickly. Besides, he was wholly absorbed in a different pursuit. It had taken him nearly a decade of living in China to become accustomed

*T'ien-pao, or "Heavenly Treasure," refers in Taoist doctrine to the ultimate level of awareness and was chosen as the name of a new era, proclaimed to honor Emperor Hsüan-tsung's conversion to Taoism.

to foreign ways; beset no longer by daily trivia, he now reveled in the pleasure of uninterrupted study. The strain of arduous study, however, had taken its toll of Fushō. His face was drawn, and his eyes, though steady, had acquired a feverish glint. Those days of torment by demands of the flesh were now in the distant past.

During this period, Fushō was surprised one day by an unexpected visit from Gōgyō. Gōgyō had withered markedly in six years. Long before, he had looked quite old for his age. He was now fifty-three or four, but he was enfeebled many years beyond his age.

Gōgyō said that he had been living at the Ch'an-ting Monastery since coming to Ch'ang-an from Lo-yang two years before. Had any other Japanese been in Ch'ang-an for two years, Fushō would surely have encountered him at some point or would have heard about him; but Gōgyō was an exception. And if one such as Gōgyō had taken the trouble to call on him, Fushō assumed correctly, then he doubtless had a matter of importance to discuss. With his task of producing textual copies nearing completion, Gōgyō was anxious to consult Fushō about a possible means of transporting the writings to Japan. His remarks were vague and uttered so softly at times as to be inaudible. Only by coaxing him to repeat again and again was Fushō able to grasp what the aging monk was trying to convey. What he could easily detect was a tone of desperation. Gōgyō told him that he had transcribed all of I-ching's translations and would soon be finishing all but the most recent of Vajrabodhi's translations of sutras of Esoteric Buddhism.

"You talk of returning, but would you go alone if passage were available?" Fushō asked.

"Certainly," Gōgyō replied, "and I'd prefer to leave as soon as possible."

Gōgyō's remark was typical of his innocence. One could seldom find a ship bound for Japan, much less one that would set sail on short notice. The eventuality of returning to Japan had not occurred to Gōgyō while he was absorbed in his task of transcribing Buddhist texts; now that his work was almost finished, however, he was unwilling to tolerate even a moment's delay in embarking on a homeward voyage.

A few days afterward, Fushō took Yōei along with him to visit Gōgyō at the Ch'an-ting Monastery. Once again they found the old monk seated at his desk, a writing brush in hand. The interior of his room was unlike what they had seen years before at the monastery in the outskirts of Lo-yang. Now, Gōgyō appeared to sit entombed among the Buddhist texts he had transcribed. Yōei and Fushō hesitated at the doorway. Countless scrolls, tied into a fantastic number of bundles and stacked high and neatly about Gōgyō's desk, formed a wall separating him from the mundane world. Every word, every phrase of these documents had been transcribed with meticulous care—a task that had taken more than thirty years.

"You should have sent back even half of what you have here when the Japanese mission left," Yōei said to him. Gōgyō's head remained bowed as he answered.

"If only I could have entrusted them to someone! But I would have had to find someone willing to cast himself into the sea if it meant saving the scriptures. I doubt whether anyone would, and so I've no choice but to take them back myself." He spoke haltingly, but with firmness, and neither Yōei nor Fushō would have injected a contradictory word.

Two days later, Yōei visited Fushō and told him about a decision he had made. His expression was serious, his words were weighted with determination.

"There are two things we must do. We must make certain all of Gōgyō's scrolls are delivered to Japan. And we must see to it that several qualified teachers of monastic discipline are sent to Japan. What other calling can there be for us? I intend to dedicate myself to fulfilling both tasks."

Fushō recalled what Gōgyō had told him the first time they met: he had foolishly wasted a good number of years study-ing; he would never have amounted to anything no matter how long he studied; he should have realized this and begun the task of transcribing Buddhist writings much earlier. Gōgyō had experienced a turnabout in what he considered to be his calling as a student-monk, and now it was Yōei, whose direction had changed. Fushō was unable to share Yōei's aspirations. He did not wish to sacrifice his own am-bitions, his desire to perfect himself as a man, for the cause of orthodox monasticism in Japan or even for the sake of Gōgyō's vast accumulation of Buddhist writings.

Yōei perceived Fushō's disinclination and said he would proceed by himself to find promising individuals and urge them to go to Japan. He reasoned that some of them might be persuaded if his own earnestness could be communicated to them.

"I have reason to believe that passage might be arranged for us," he added. A monk by the name of Tao-k'ang was in residence at Ta-an-kuo-ssu, where Yōei was lodging. Tao-k'ang was the Buddhist minister for the household of Lin Tsung. Lin Tsung was the elder brother of Li Lin-fu, prime minister of the empire. Yōei had a plan. He would try to obtain a ship by addressing a request through Tao-k'ang to Lin Tsung and, ultimately, to Premier Li Lin-fu.

Fushō in time agreed to cooperate with Yōei, but for a reason of his own. For more than a year, he had been worried about his health. The slightest physical exertion would bring on extreme fatigue. He often became feverish. Yōei thought this might be the result of excessive study, but Fushō suspected other causes.

Burdened with serious doubts about his own health, Fushō dared not part company with Yōei and remain alone on the continent. He thought he should return to Japan if it were at all possible, for he could not know when the next Japanese embassy would arrive in China.

In less than a month's time, Yōei had approached four monks from among his acquaintances and succeeded in persuading them to travel to Japan. One was Tao-k'ang, whose aid Yōei had hoped to enlist in order to procure a ship. Tao-k'ang became fascinated with the thought of going to a foreign country when he heard Yōei's description of the forthcoming venture. The others were Ch'eng-kuan of Ch'ang-an, Te-ch'ing of Lo-yang, and the Korean monk Ju-hai from Koguryō. All were Buddhists with whom Yōei had become acquainted since his arrival in Ch'ang-an.

Tao-k'ang's joining them, unexpected as it was, proved to be felicitous. Not only would he serve as the link to Premier Li Lin-fu, but also to his teacher, the eminent monk Ganjin

Ganjin

of Yang-chou, who might be prevailed upon to recommend from among his many disciples several qualified administrators of monastic vows. Tao-k'ang, Ch'eng-kuan, Te-chi'ng, and Ju-hai had devoted many years to the study of the *Vinaya* but were not yet qualified to administer vows. Thus there was the need to enlist yet other Buddhists of proven scholarly and moral attainment.

Shortly thereafter, through Tao-k'ang's intercession, Yōei and Fushō met Lin Tsung, who in turn presented the Japanese to his brother, the prime minister. Li, thirty-nine at the time, was a member of T'ang royalty. He had begun his career as a low-ranking official, but after finding an ally in the imperial consort, who brought him to the notice of Emperor Hsüan-tsung, he had risen swiftly to the position of prime minister. He was then at the zenith of his ministerial career. "Sly and alert by nature, he has a tongue that is honeyed, and a belly with a dagger ever poised beside it." Such was his reputation. He resorted to any means—intrigue, scheming, conspiracy, or brute authority—to attain his ends and was eventually to sow the seeds of decay that would spread throughout the great empire of T'ang. Being a man of this nature, he was quick to understand their problem and to devise a facile solution.

Li Lin-fu's thin lips and cold eyes were set in a face wholly without expression. As he answered their request for help in finding passage back to Japan, he kept his gaze fixed on a remote point in the distance.

"Ostensibly you will be transporting offerings to Mount T'ien-t'ai and traveling by sea owing to the difficulty of moving goods overland. A favorable wind will enable you to sail straight for Japan. Should adverse winds bring you back to our coast, your official papers will identify you as emissaries to Mount T'ien-t'ai."

In the presence of the Japanese monks, he scribbled a note that was neither a letter of introduction nor a message of command. Addressed to Li Tsou, a military commander in the Rice Administration in Yang-chou, it simply stated, "Construct a large vessel, stock it with provisions, and deliver it to the bearer of this note."

Yōei and Fushō decided it might be best to leave Ch'ang-an later in the year. As they expected, Genrō agreed to go with them. Gōgyō, however, left immediately for Lo-yang. Before setting sail, he would have to bring together the vast number of Buddhist texts he had left in idle storage in various monasteries. He would rejoin the others in Yang-chou at the Ta-ming Monastery.

7

In 742 Yōei, Fushō, and Genrō left Ch'ang-an, where they had spent six years, accompanied by three monks of China and a fourth from the Korean kingdom of Koguryō. The party of Buddhists traveled overland to Pien-chou, then sailed the Grand Canal directly to Yang-chou, gliding past landscapes already bleak and wintry. The age-old willow trees lining the banks were yellowed, and reeds stood broken and wilted at the water's edge.

Yōei seldom spoke once they were aboard the craft. He sat in silence over long stretches of time, his arms folded and his thoughts to himself. He was beguiled by an entirely new dream, the possibility of persuading the great Ganjin himself to go to Japan as a teacher of monastic discipline. He would have no regrets leaving China with his studies uncompleted if he could realize this dream as well as fulfill the self-imposed mission of transporting to Japan the sacred writings that had taken Gōgyō a lifetime to transcribe. His own aspirations would be of trifling importance by comparison. Yōei was excited by the thought of taking a precious treasure from the great empire of T'ang, but his expression for some reason reflected moodiness rather than exhilaration.

Fushō's thoughts were weighted with gloom as they neared Yang-chou. He regretted leaving China. He regretted leaving behind Ch'ang-an, the Ch'ung-fu Monastery, and the uncounted scrolls of scriptures he had not yet read. Genrō was assailed alternately by a nostalgic yearning for Japan, which became intense the moment he boarded the vessel, and by his fear of a voyage across the open sea. He appeared listless.

The party arrived at Yang-chou in late October. Exceeded in size only by Ch'ang-an and Lo-yang, Yang-chou was the site of the Great Metropolitan Constabulary and the headquarters of the Magistrate of Huai-nan Province.* No sooner had the monks changed their garments at the Chi-ch'i Monastery than they were off to the Ta-ming Monastery in order to meet with Ganjin.

The city of Yang-chou was divided into two zones. The Little City, built on a rise, consisted of rows of government offices including that of the Huai-nan magistrate. Spread out in a rectangle over the flat land in the south was the commercial area known as the Big City. The Ta-ming-ssu was a large monastery situated in the southwest corner of the Little City; a cluster of imposing halls of worship stood in prominence on one side of the spacious grounds, and a nine-storied pagoda on the other. It was there the Japanese met with Ganjin.

Arrayed behind Ganjin in the room were some thirty monks. At the age of fifty-five, Ganjin was a large man of sturdy physique. He had a broad forehead, large eyes and nose, and a generous mouth, solidly set; the crown of his head rose prominently, and there was determination in the set of his jaw. Fushō detected a quality reminiscent of the Japanese warrior in the celebrated monk. Ganjin was a Buddhist singularly dedicated to monastic discipline and a teacher reputedly without peer in the region south of the Huai River and west of the Yangtze Estuary.

Tao-k'ang presented the members of the party to Ganjin. Then Yōei, speaking in their behalf, explained that Buddhism in its eastward flow had reached the shores of Japan and the Law of Buddha was being propagated, but that the Japanese had yet to welcome a monk who could administer the monastic vows to them; and he asked Ganjin to favor them with recommendations of qualified teachers of monasticism. Yōei spoke of Prince Shōtoku. The Prince had prophesied a vigorous flourishing of Buddha's teaching in two hundred years' time, and the fulfillment of the prophecy seemed imminent. He spoke also of Prince Toneri, then living in Japan, of his devotion to Buddhism, of his fervent wish for the establishment of orthodoxy in Japan.

Ganjin responded immediately. There was a surprisingly soft ring to the voice that came from this large figure and a

*The area between the Huai and Yangtze rivers in east-central China.

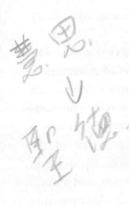

fascinating quality about the flow of words and the assurance it inspired.

"Hear what I have been told. When the sage Hui-ssu of South Mountain died long ago, he was reincarnated as a prince of the land of Yamato that he might spread the teaching of Buddha and lift the people out of darkness. I have been told, too, that Prince Nagaya of the Japanese nation revered the Buddha's Law. The Prince had a thousand clerical vestments made to be distributed among virtuous monks in our nation. Embroidered on each robe was this quatrain:

> Though our lands, the mountains and streams, are
>   not one,
> We share the same winds, the moon, the heavens.
> Let the bodhisattvas hear of this
> That we may in another life be united.

Japan is surely a country where Buddhism is destined to flourish. The Japanese have expressed their wish. Who amongst you will cross the sea to transmit the codes of monasticism?"

No one answered. After an interval of silence, a monk named Hsiang-yen came forward and spoke.

"I have been told that one must cross a vast expanse of dark green waters in order to reach Japan and that of a hundred sailings not one is ever successful. To acquire life as a human being is rare good fortune, and to be born in China is also rare good fortune. It is so explained in the *Nirvana Sutra*."

"Is there no one who will go?" Ganjin asked, interrupting Hsiang-yen. There were no replies. Then Ganjin spoke a third time. "It will be for the good of Buddhism. True, Japan lies beyond a vast expanse of dark green waters. But a Buddhist should not be reluctant to risk his life. Since none of you will go, I shall." A hush fell over the room. The decision had been made.

Only Yōei among the visitors had had an opportunity to speak. As he sat quietly listening, Fushō suddenly felt himself transported. The monks, more than thirty, sat with their heads bowed, a sign of acquiescence. Ganjin called out names of individuals. As the names were called, heads were raised in response. When seventeen faces were uplifted, Ganjin lapsed into silence. All had been decided during those moments. Ganjin would cross the sea to Japan accompanied by seventeen disciples of high attainment.

The Japanese monks and their companions set out to return to the Chi-ch'i Monastery, where they had taken up quarters. The high ground on which the Ta-ming Monastery stood commanded a panorama of the Big City. The Grand Canal coursed from north to south through the center of Yang-chou and was intersected by twelve avenues that ran east to west. Fushō recalled having read a verse that contained a line: in this city, even the earth exudes perfume. The twenty-four bridges that spanned the many rivers, the roofs of the storehouses lining the banks of the Grand Canal, the clusters of Buddhist edifices, even the trees and shrubbery covering the open spaces—all glistened coldly in the winter sun and seemed to Fushō to exude perfume. He was still possessed by the ecstasy he had entered while at the Ta-ming Monastery.

The Chi-ch'i Monastery, south of the city, became the center of activity for the monks as they began that very day their preparations for the voyage. Gōgyō arrived in Yang-chou two weeks after the others and came straight to the Chi-ch'i Monastery. He was accompanied by three haulers and two pack horses bearing his possessions.

On the day Gōgyō joined them, the four Japanese, three Chinese, and one Korean monk separated into smaller groups to be lodged in monasteries on the outskirts of the city. They did so in order to evade government surveillance. The return voyage of the four Japanese monks would itself be an undertaking of extralegal character. The sailing of more than twenty Chinese for Japan—Ganjin's party of eighteen and Tao-k'ang's group of four—would not be overtly sanctioned. The preparations would have to be carried out under cover of secrecy.

Yōei alone remained at the Chi-ch'i Monastery, their headquarters, with the expectation that Ganjin would join him there eventually. Fushō and Gōgyō moved to the Ta-ming, and Genrō to the K'ai-yüan Monastery.

Yōei and Fushō worked together daily to make ready for

the voyage. The terse directive from Premier Li Lin-fu was instrumental in their obtaining the assistance of Li Tsou of the Rice Administration. A ship for their use would be built at Tung-ho at the estuary of the Yangtze. Fushō and others learned afterward that Li Tsou was a nephew of Li Lin-fu and that the premier had assigned members of his clan to important posts in military units within the Rice Administration. Li Tsou was also renowned as a painter and is evaluated thus in the ninth-century *Record of Famous Painters in History*: "His brushstrokes fall haphazardly. His paintings achieve the ultimate in beauty." Some years later he was to become a victim of the political upheaval that followed the death of Li Lin-fu and be reduced to an insignificant county prefect of Hsiang-shan in Ming-chou.

The monks thought it best to await the fair winds of spring of the coming year, 743. They spent the intervening period accumulating food and other supplies, which they stored at the Chi-ch'i Monastery.

*   *   *   *   *   *   *   *   *

Ganjin was born into a family with the surname of Shun-yü in Chiang-yang County in Yang-chou in 688, the fourth year of the rule of Empress Wu. The year corresponds to the second in the reign of Empress Jitō in Japan.

The histories tell us nothing about Ganjin's childhood. When Empress Wu deposed the sovereign of the T'ang empire, instituted the dynastic title of Chou, and herself occupied the throne, Ganjin was two years old. Ganjin's father had taken his monastic vows and studied the doctrine of Zen under Chih-man of the Ta-yün Monastery in Yang-chou. Ganjin was thirteen when he first accompanied his father to the Ta-yün Monastery. He was deeply moved by a statue of the Buddha and sought his father's permission to enter the clergy. He was made an acolyte under the tutelage of Chih-man at the Ta-yün, and was assigned subsequently to the Lung-hsing Monastery.

In 705, Ganjin, then seventeen, had the Vow of Bodhisattvas administered to him by the teacher of the *Vinaya*, Tao-en. At the age of nineteen, he took up the ringed staff of the pilgrim and traveled first to Lo-yang, then to Ch'ang-an.

He was twenty when he ascended the ordination platform at Shih-chi-ssu in Ch'ang-an and took the Supreme Clerical Vow. Shih-chi-ssu occupied the southwest corner of the Ta-p'ing Quarter, west of the Great Vermilion-Bird Thoroughfare. It was the monastery where Chi-ts'ang, the learned monk of the Three Treatises Sect, had spent his last years and where the renowned Ch'an-tao of the Pure Land Sect had delivered his sermons. The vow was administered by the teacher of the *Vinaya*, Hung-ching, of Nan-ch'üan Monastery in Ching-chou. Hung-ching was the monk, held in devout reverence at the imperial court, who had thrice responded to requests from Empress Wu and her successor, Emperor Chung-tsung, to betake himself from monastic seclusion to the palace in order to administer Buddhist vows.

The young Ganjin devoted himself wholly to the study of the *Tripitaka** during his sojourn in the twin capitals of the empire. Under the direction of Yung-ch'i, he studied Tao-i's *Manual of Vinaya Sect Rituals, Commentary on the Karma*, and *Principles of Relative Merit*, and under the tutelage of I-wei he studied the *Annotation of the Vinaya Canon* by Fa-li. He also attended lectures on Fa-li's *Annotation*, given by Yüan-chih at Hsi-ming-ssu and by Ta-liang at Kuan-yin-ssu in Ch'ang-an. There is little biographical information on Yung-ch'i and I-wei. We know, however, that both were disciples, as were Yüan-chih and Fa-li, of the distinguished scholar of the West Tower Sect, Man-i, and that they were prominent in their time.

In 713, Ganjin, then twenty-five, ascended the teacher's platform for the first time and lectured on the *Annotation of the Vinaya Canon*. Some time later he returned to his home south of the Huai River. When he was thirty, he lectured on the *Manual of Vinaya Sect Rituals* and *Principles of Relative Merit;* at thirty-nine he lectured on the *Commentary on the Karma*. During his lifetime he gave forty lectures on the *Vinaya* and commentaries, seventy on the *Manual,* and ten each on the *Principles of Relative Merit* and *Commentary on the Karma*. He administered the tonsure and monastic vows to more than forty thousand persons.

*The three-part compendium of Buddhist scriptures, of which the Vinaya scriptures constitute a part.

The only extant description of Ganjin during this productive period of his life is this passage in the *Record of the Eastward Journey of the Great Monk of T'ang*:* "He alone preached as a mendicant in the region between the rivers Huai and Yangtze. He promoted Buddhism and enlightened the people. His uncounted accomplishments cannot possibly be related in detail."

8

Preparations for the voyage were virtually complete when the new year of 743 arrived. The monks planned to sail with the first favorable wind at the beginning of March, for the ship would then be ready.

In March, however, the coastal waters off T'ai-chou, Wen-chou, and Ming-chou were infested with pirates, and the sea routes were closed to both government and private ships. Although the vessel was built, the voyage had to be postponed. Thus March went by. Toward the end of April, Tao-k'ang sought out Yōei to sound a note of warning.

"We're undertaking this voyage in order to take the codes of monastic discipline to Japan. Even though we're supposed to be Buddhists of proven religious attainment and moral purity, we have Ju-hai with us. Ju-hai has been deplorably lax in his conduct, and he's not a learned man. Shouldn't we exclude him?"

Although Tao-k'ang had given an accurate description of the Korean monk Ju-hai, neither Yōei nor Fushō took heed of his warning. Not long after, government officials came to search the monasteries where the Japanese monks were in residence. Nettled by the possibility of being left behind, Ju-hai had gone to the magistrate and denounced Tao-k'ang as a pirate chieftain, and the Japanese monks as cohorts.

On the day following the search, constables descended on the monasteries. Fushō, Gōgyō, and Genrō were surprised in their sleep and promptly taken into custody. Yōei slipped away and lay concealed in the pond at the Chi-ch'i Monastery, but was soon taken capitve and led away in his drenched state. Although Tao-k'ang escaped and went into hiding in

*An account of Ganjin's travels written by a disciple in 799, thirty-six years after his death.

the city, he, too, was found and taken into custody the next day.

An extensive investigation followed the discovery of a quantity of provisions at the Chi-ch'i Monastery and disclosure of the fact that the monks had had a ship constructed. The authorities refused to accept Yōei and Fushō's explanation of their intent to take the sea route to the Kuo-ch'ing Monastery at Mount T'ien-t'ai. The letter from the prime minister to Li Tsou ultimately cleared the monks of the charge of piracy, but they were still kept under arrest. Ju-hai, for his crime of slander, was given sixty strokes of the cane, banished from the clergy, and deported.

The authorities at Yang-chou sought instructions from the central government regarding action to be taken on the four Japanese monks. The matter was referred to the Hung-lu Office in Ch'ang-an, which administered the affairs of visiting foreign clerics. An inquiry sent from the Hung-lu Office to the Great Fu-hsien Monastery in Lo-yang, where Fushō and Yōei and the others had resided initially, elicited this reply: "The monks in question left with the Emperor's cortege in 736 and have not since returned," The name of Gōgyō was unaccountably missing from their register.

Officials at the Hung-lu office based their report to the central government on the information received from the Great Fu-hsien Monastery, and in due time the following edict was sent down to Yang-chou: "Yōei and the others are foreign monks who came to the empire for purposes of study. They have each been receiving twenty-five bolts of silk annually and a set of clothes at each seasonal change; furthermore, they were accorded the privilege of departing with the Emperor's entourage. There has been no deception or misappropriation. Now they wish to return to their country. Release them and grant them the freedom to leave as they wish. Dispatch them with care as would befit the custom of Yang-chou."

Clearly this favorable outcome was due to the intercession of Premier Li Lin-fu. The monks had been imprisoned in April; it was August when they were released. They would continue to receive government sustenance, and the magistrate of Yang-chou would oversee their departure at such time as passage would be available. Meanwhile, the four Japanese were given lodging in private homes.

The plan to sail for Japan collapsed in the wake of this unexpected incident. Soon after their release, Yōei and Fushō called secretly on Ganjin at the Ta-ming Monastery in order to persuade him to consider yet another attempt. Ganjin was still determined to sail for Japan, and he even gave them words of encouragement. They were not to be daunted, he told them, for such a turn of events was by no means uncommon. He would somehow find a way to fulfill his vow to cross the seas to Japan. Discretion dictated their abandoning the ship and provisions, but they would begin at once to prepare anew.

Although Ganjin's determination had not wavered, unexpectedly two men among the original group decided to quit. One was Tao-k'ang, who had become totally disenchanted. He asked to be excused for reasons of health, gathered up his belongings, and left hurriedly for Ch'ang-an.

The other was Genrō. At first he told them that a voyage on a small vessel would be perilous and that he would postpone his sailing until the next embassy came from Japan. There was no question about his desire to return to Japan, but he wanted no part of what he considered a reckless, foolhardy venture. This was his real reason, and he said as much when he appeared at the magistrate's office in order to obtain permission to leave Yang-chou and return to Ch'ang-an. For this he was berated by Yōei: why couldn't Genrō board the same ship as Ganjin, who was willing to be seaborne though it meant risking his life? But Fushō was able to quiet Yōei, and the monks were able to gather for a feast to bid farewell to Genrō, who alone, among them, would remain on Chinese soil.

During the dinner, yet another person announced his withdrawal from the venture. It was Gōgyō. "I think I'll wait for another opportunity," he said, his voice little more than a murmur. "If I'm aboard a ship with Ganjin, everyone will be concerned first and above all with Ganjin, and quite naturally so, he being the accomplished monk-scholar he is. This is what worries me." From this rather cryptic statement neither Yōei nor Fushō could deduce his cause for worry.

They understood only that Gōgyō refused to sail with them. They said nothing, for they knew there was no changing Gōgyō's mind once it had been made up.

A few days afterward, Fushō found the opportunity to ask Gōgyō about his reasons. Looking distraught, Gōgyō explained why he had decided not to sail with them: should the ship ever be in danger of foundering, everyone would be so concerned with Ganjin's safety that the sacred texts might well be abandoned; and so he could not allow the precious scrolls to be taken aboard the same ship. Fushō could not assure him it would be otherwise, for he would himself elect to save Ganjin under those circumstances.

When Yōei was informed of Gōgyō's concern, he pondered the matter briefly, then told Fushō that he agreed with Gōgyō.

"Ganjin is precious," Yōei said, "but so is that vast collection of sacred writings. If we're convinced that both are equally precious to Japan, then we should abide by Gōgyō's suggestion and see to it that his texts are carried on another ship."

A few days afterward, Fushō helped Gōgyō move his belongings to his new quarters, in the Ch'an-chih Monastery. Gōgyō would remain in Yang-chou and await passage aboard some other ship. From a corner of the grounds of the Ch'an-chih Monastery, one could see the Grand Canal, which coursed along the foot of the rise. Countless vessels of every imaginable size choked the canal; and on each of them ship hands could be seen scurrying about, shouting lustily.

Gōgyō's new room was much brighter than those he had occupied in Lo-yang and Ch'ang-an. He would again be engrossed in the work of transcribing sutras until the day another ship set sail for Japan. Remembering how chilled Gōgyō often appeared as he sat beside his desk, Fushō was especially gratified to know that the aged monk would be occupying a room that admitted sunlight.

Autumn sped past and soon it was winter, an unusually warm one that year. It did not snow in the area of Yang-chou. Preparations for the voyage progressed steadily. The cost was to be borne by Ganjin, who provided the monks with eighty strings of coins. With that money they were able to purchase a naval vessel from Liu Chu-lin, magistrate of Ling-nan Province,* hire eighteen sea hands, and stock the ship with provisions. Liu gave them possession of the ship in December, precisely when the pirate Wu Ling-kuang was making frequent raids on Yung-chia County and when warning flares were blazing along the entire Chekiang coast. A curious man, they thought, to relinquish a naval vessel at such a time. Indeed, Liu Chu-lin years later was to pay with his life for malfeasance.

The atmosphere in the Ta-ming Monastery became charged with excitement that December. Ganjin was to be accompanied by Hsiang-yen, Tao-hsing, Te-ch'ing, Ssu-ch'a, and others. There would be seventeen monks, including Yōei and Fushō—a few less than the previous time. There would, in addition, be jade-workers, artists, sculptors, embroiderers, and other artisans. With the crew, the voyagers would number one hundred and eighty-five.

The amount and quality of the commodities Ganjin had gathered together for shipment to Japan was impressive: of Buddhist texts, the *Avataṃsaka Sūtra*, the *Greater Prajñā-pāramitā Sūtra*, the *Mahāsaṃghāta Sūtra*, and the *Greater Nirvana Sūtra*, all inscribed in gold, and one hundred other sutras and commentaries; of Buddhist images, a painting of the Five Buddhas of Wisdom and another of the Bejeweled Buddha, one gold-encrusted statue, and a six-panel screen depicting Buddhas and bodhisattvas; of ceremonial equipment, panels displaying the lunar calendric and solar cyclic charts, one hundred and twenty Bodhimandala banners, fourteen beaded banners, eight hand-banners with jade rings, fifty sutra containers inlaid with mother-of-pearl, twenty copper jars, twenty-four floral rugs, one thousand clerical stoles, one thousand clerical robes, one thousand chairs, four large copper canopies, forty bamboo-leaf canopies, twenty large copper basins as well as twenty more of intermediate size and forty-four of a smaller size, eighty copper plates measuring a foot in diameter and two hundred

---

*Approximately the area of Kwangtung and Kwangsi provinces in south China today.

more of a smaller dimension, sixteen white rattan baskets, and six polychrome rattan baskets.

Of medicines and aromatics, twenty globules of musk, and more than six hundred pounds in all of aloeswood, onycha, valerian, camphor, a perfume called *tan-t'ang*, benzoin, light aloeswood, essence of sweet basil, costusroot, and frankincense; some five hundred pounds of myrobalan, pepper, asafetida, crystal sugar, and sugar cane; forty gallons of bee's honey; and eighty bundles of sugarcane stalks. Included also were such items as ten thousand strings of bronze coins, another ten thousand of *cheng-lu* coins, five thousand strings of *tzu-pien* coins, twenty gauze hoods, and thirty linen shoes.

All preparations were at last complete. The vessel was laden to overflowing with men and cargo when she set sail, unnoticed, from Yang-chou on a bright moonlit night late in December.

When the crew unfurled the sail, the ship coursed easily down the great Yangtze to the sea. As it approached Lang-kou-p'u (T'ai-ts'ang in Kiangsu Province), though, the moon began to take on a red cast as an ill wind sent swirls of dust into the air and raised high swells. The men decided then to lie at anchor offshore for the night. As the ship approached the beach, however, its prow was torn open by the pounding waves and seawater invaded the hold. Everyone was forced to go ashore. The tide rose and soon the beach was inundated. Ganjin was lifted onto a reed stack by Yōei, Fushō, and Ssu-ch'a while everyone else stood in sea water through the night. The piercing wind, which persisted all night, and the chill from the water seemed to penetrate to their very marrow.

The following day was calm. The voyagers were able to repair the damage, and their vessel was again seaborne. They proceeded as far as Ta-pan-shan (one of the Ma-an Islands) but finally could not moor the ship because of high waves. They sailed on to Hsia-yü-shan, where they lay at anchor for a month.

When the wind again favored them, they set sail for Sang-shih-shan (an island in the Chü-shan Archipelago). They managed to approach the island despite the rough sea but could not pass through the rocks lining the shore and were forced to veer back out toward deeper waters. They could not negotiate the move successfully. The waves carried the ship to and fro, out to the deep, then back toward shore. This continued for several hours, and ultimately the vessel was caught fast on the rocks. Half of the men managed to get off. The others were still on board when the ship rode a breaker on to the beach and broke into several pieces.

When dawn came, they saw that all the cargo had been washed away. There was no food or water. Trapped on a barren strip at the foot of soaring coastal cliffs, the one hundred and eighty-five men spent the next three days tormented by thirst and hunger.

On the third day, the wind had spent its force, the sky was again a mild expanse of blue, and the winter sun shone wanly on the strange aspect of the marooned. Toward dusk of the fourth day, they were discovered by a crew of fishermen, who could provide them with rice and water.

On the evening of the fifth day, a coastal patrol ship came to the island; the officers asked them about their mishap and then sailed away. Three days afterward, the voyagers sighted a government vessel approaching the island. It was forty days since their departure from Yang-chou when the crew and passengers were taken off the sandy strip onto the ship. Settled comfortably on deck, the one hundred and eighty-five men no longer looked desperate; they appeared content as they stared vacantly out to sea, speaking not a word to one another. As the vessel sailed back to the continent, it passed among an incredible number of islets dotting the surface. The sea was calm, and the voyagers could scarcely imagine that this was the very sea that had tossed their ship about like a leaf and dashed it to pieces, carrying away everything in it and leaving the castaways on an inhospitable beach. Nothing was left of the vast cargo, the sutras, sacred images, ceremonial accouterments, medicines and incense. All of it had been swallowed by the sea.

That they had not taken on Gōgyō's scrolls as cargo was a consolation to Fushō. Had Gōgyō been with them, the product of years of selfless endeavor on the Asian mainland would have vanished, like the foam of waves, into the sea. As Fushō mused, Yōei spoke to him.

"Ganjin is still intent on going to Japan. It seems we're to be taken to the King Aśoka Monastery in Mou-shan. Ganjin says he will plan another voyage while we're there."

Fushō could scarcely believe what he heard. They had barely come through with their lives, and already Ganjin and Yōei were laying plans for another sailing. Surely they were the only ones. Sitting near the prow, Ganjin was wrapped in garments provided by the crew; attending him closely were Hsiang-yen, Ssu-ch'a, and Tao-hsing—the three who, like shadows, were constantly by his side. Except for Ganjin, almost everyone was half-naked. The cold sea breeze of late January did not allow their bodies even a moment's respite from trembling. The bare castaways, who filled the government vessel beyond capacity, were being transported to the coast of Ming-chou (Ning-po in Chekiang Province).

Once again the one hundred and eighty-five were back on the Asian mainland. They had set off from Yang-chou and sailed down the Yangtze River; their ship had been tossed about by the turbulent sea as it drifted aimlessly about the Ma-an Islands at the Yangtze Estuary. The government vessel that picked them up had threaded its way back through the maze of the Chou-shan Islands and deposited them in a corner of the Bay of K'ang-chou. There the party waited at a seaside village while the governor of Ming-chou sought instructions from the central government. After twenty days a directive was received: most of the voyagers were ordered to return to their native provinces, but the seventeen monks were to be detained at the King Aśoka Monastery.

Ming-chou, previously a part of Yüeh-chou, became independent in 728. It comprised four districts—Mou-shan, Feng-hua, Tz'u-chi, and Weng-shan.* The ancient King Aśoka Monastery, situated some fourteen miles east of the administrative center of Mou-shan, was set against a backdrop of low hills. Its spacious grounds were shaded by groves of bamboo. The original buildings had been destroyed by fire one hundred and seventy years before,† and what had been rebuilt

---

*In the T'ang period, the province (tao) was subdivided into territorial administrative units called chou. "Districts" (hsien) were subdivisions of the chou.

†In 576.

—smaller and now fallen into disrepair—did little to evoke the monastery's former magnificence. Nonetheless, many of the old stories and legends about the monastery had survived.

The monastery was named for its prized possession, the King Aśoka Stupa. Tradition had it that King Aśoka of India had put deities to work in order to have eighty-four thousand stupas made in commemoration of the one hundredth anniversary of the death of Śākya Buddha and that all the stupas lay buried in the ground. The small stupa in the monastery was said to be one of the eighty-four thousand.

Yōei and Fushō were acquainted with the story associating the origin of the monastery with the King Aśoka Stupa. In 265, or the first year of the Western Chin Dynasty, a certain Liu Sa-k'o of Ping-chou was transported in death to the infernal realm of Yama-rāja and brought to trial for his earthly sins; when he was living he had hunted often in the hills, riding his sorrel and sending his falcon aloft to capture wild game. Because death had claimed him before the expiration of his natural span of life, Liu Sa-k'o was allowed to return to the world of the living on the condition that he enter the Buddhist clergy and look for a King Aśoka stupa. Liu became a monk when he was restored to life, and his search for a King Aśoka stupa brought him to Mou-shan. Hearing the peal of a bell emanating nightly from a spot in the ground, he dug into it and there found the precious stupa. The monastery was built over that site.

The stupa stood a scant foot-and-a-half high on a base eight inches square. Fushō saw it many times in the reliquary. Once, he and Ssu-ch'a had gone together to look at it. Ssu-ch'a, then twenty, was the youngest member of the party, but his brilliance made him worthy of the special regard in which Ganjin held him. Scrupulous by nature, he customarily made a detailed record of everything he saw or heard about. This is his description of the King Aśoka Stupa: "The stupa is made not of gold, jade, stone, earth, copper, or iron. Its color is dark purple. Engraved on the four sides are depictions of Jātaka tales.* Its spire does not have a 'dew-catching' plate at the base. A bell is suspended inside it."

*Stories of the many previous births and incarnations of Śākya Buddha contained in the Buddhist scriptures.

Although Ssu-ch'a described the color as dark purple, Fushō thought it was a much lighter shade. But, as Ssu-ch'a had indicated, the stupa seemed to be made of a rare, unknown substance. Whenever Fushō peered inside it and saw the suspended bell, he wondered if it was the legendary bell that had sounded out from underground.

Fushō and Ssu-ch'a took every opportunity to stroll about the vicinity of the monastery. The handsome young monk continued to cram his notebook with details of everything he saw, quite as if that were his given mission. An imprint of the right foot of a Buddha was visible on the top of a hill located approximately a mile southeast of the monastery; another, of the left foot, was set in a boulder on high ground situated about a mile northeast of the monastery. The imprints were identical in size—seventeen inches long, seven inches wide across the ball of the foot, and five inches across the heel. Each impression was four inches deep. The thousand-spoked wheel was clearly discernible in both, identifying them as footprints of the Buddha Kāśyapa.*

Situated about a half-mile east of the monastery was a roadside well, only three feet deep, which gave forth spring water. There were many curious stories about this well. It never overflowed despite heavy rain, nor did it dry up in times of drought. It was the lair of an eel eighteen-inches long, which local inhabitants believed to be the manifestation of a guardian bodhisattva of the King Aśoka Stupa. That the eel was visible only to those who were blessed was quite generally accepted. So also was the legend that a protective roof overlaid with precious gems had once been placed over the well but had been washed away immediately by a sudden gush of well water.

One story was often recounted at the monastery. In 645, or a century before, a monk known as Min came to the monastery in the company of hundreds of disciples. The monk lectured for a month on the scriptures, and local people gathered every evening to hear him. One night, everyone present witnessed a strange assemblage of some one hundred outlandish Buddhist monks walking about the stupa. The min-

*The last of the seven Buddhas who appeared on earth countless eons before the birth of Śākya Buddha.

iature stupa and the midget Chu-ju* men circling around
it were so magnified in the eyes of the onlookers that they
assumed natural proportions, a phenomenon that seemed not
in the least unusual. The queer occurrence was reported to a
monk at the monastery, and he was said to have told the people: "There is no reason whatever to consider this sight unusual. Every year people from near and far gather here on
the days of the four major Buddhist festivities, and always at
midnight those monks are seen circumambulating the stupa,
chanting a sutra, and praising the virtues of the Buddha."
Fushō was enchanted with the account of this nocturnal
parade of monks. More than any other legend associated with
the monastery, this one concerning the Chu-ju monks walking round and round the stupa conjured up a scene that was
strange but believable.

Ganjin and the sixteen monks welcomed the new year at
King Aśoka Monastery. About the time the spring sun had
begun to brighten the sparse bamboo groves of the deserted
grounds, Ganjin was invited to lecture on the *Vinaya* and administer monastic vows at the Lung-hsing Monastery in
Yüeh-chou. He agreed promptly to the request. Yōei and Fushō were among those selected to accompany Ganjin to
Yüeh-chou. On their return travel the monks visited K'ang-
chou, Hu-chou, and Hsüan-chou, and in each of those places
Ganjin administered the monastic vows to many. They returned to the King Aśoka Monastery at the end of summer.

The experience of accompanying Ganjin brought Yōei and
Fushō a totally new kind of learning. For the first time since
their arrival in China ten years before, they departed from the
conventional path of independent study and acquired a teacher. They heard Ganjin lecture on the *Vinaya* many times over,
and each time they discovered something new in what he
said. Ganjin's own teacher, Tao-an, had been in residence
at the Lung-hsing Monastery in Yüeh-chou, and Ganjin's
deportment during their stay there mirrored a respectful
humility which the Japanese observed closely. At the K'ai-
yüan Monastery, also in Yüeh-chou, they had the opportunity to hear words of counsel imparted by the eminent

*According to ancient Chinese histories, a race of dark-skinned midgets
in Southeast Asia.

T'an-i, who had studied with Ganjin. At the Lung-hsing Monastery of K'ang-chou they were able to meet with Ling-i, a ranking disciple of Ganjin's senior colleague, Fa-shen.

Shortly after their return, the monks were faced with a predicament. The clerics of Yüeh-chou had learned about the projected voyage and, in an attempt to prevent Ganjin from leaving China, had asked the *chou* officials to apprehend Yōei, the man responsible for the scheme. Yōei sensed danger and concealed himself in the home of one Wang Chi but was soon taken into custody. Fushō, too, went into hiding, though he was not sought.

Yōei was shackled about the neck, put under guard, and sent off to the capital. Yet he was back within a month's time. He told the other monks that someone had agreed to forge a report on his behalf, enabling him to escape at K'ang-chou. The report was to state that he had become ill, was released pending recovery, then died later in the year.

The episode had an electric effect on the group, and thereafter preparations for the voyage moved rapidly. In the beginning of autumn, Fa-chin and two other monks left secretly for Fu-chou, where they were to purchase a ship and stock it with provisions.

Two weeks later, Ganjin led a party of thirty monks and attendants in an exodus from Ming-chou. They worshipped at the King Aśoka Stupa, offered prayers at the miraculous well on behalf of the bodhisattva in the form of an eel, visited the footprints left by the Buddha of a primeval era, and then departed by a road that would take them across the mountains to T'ai-chou. At the outskirts of Mou-shan, they were met by Lu T'ung-tsai, then governor of Ming-chou, and a host of monks, who had gathered to bid farewell to the men who had lived a year in their midst. The travelers were given food for the journey and assigned escorts to accompany them as far as the Po-tu-ts'un Monastery. After their arrival at Po-tu-ts'un, Ganjin urged that a damaged pagoda be repaired and called upon the people to construct a hall of worship.

The party arrived at T'ai-chou and spent a night at the Po-ch'üan Monastery in Ning-hai County. On the following morning, they began their journey to T'ien-t'ai Mountain,

the most hallowed of Buddhist grounds within the empire.
The route of travel was long and precipitòus. Snow began to
fall after dusk and soon became a blinding flurry. The monks
spent the following day trudging over ridges and through
valleys; at sundown they arrived at their destination, the Kuo-
ch'ing Monastery.

At T'ien-t'ai Mountain, Yōei and Fushō felt as though they
were back amidst the mountains of their native Japan. The
crests of the receding layers of mountains were covered with
a dense growth of pines, oaks, and camphors.

There were seventy-two monasteries in these mountains.
True to its fame as one of the four marvels of the empire, the
Kuo-ch'ing, which lay nestled among five peaks, was in
every sense hallowed Buddhist ground enfolded in an atmosphere of fathomless mystery. The monastery was bordered
on both sides by streams, which converged in front of it.

The monks spent three days at the Kuo-ch'ing Monastery
visiting the many sacred sites in the mountains. With wonder
they regarded the grandeur and beauty of pagodas and temples that came into relief in quick succession—in valleys, atop
ridges, or amidst dense forests. They realized then that only
an infinitesimal part of the wonder of this place had been
described in "The Ode to T'ien-t'ai Mountain," a poem by
Sun Ch'o, which had made T'ien-t'ai a name celebrated in
every corner of the empire.

When the monks left T'ien-t'ai Mountain, they traveled
through the Shih-feng District to Lin-hai, and trekked sheer
ridges for several days before descending to the plain. They
followed the Ling River downstream to the coastal Huang-
yen District and from there took the government highway
that ran along the seacoast toward Yung-chia County (in
Wen-chou). This would be their last station before arriving
at Fu-chou, where they were to meet the three who had left
Mou-shan before them.

When they stopped for a night's lodging at a monastery
named Ch'an-lin-ssu, the monks were surprised by invading
officials who carried a warrant issued by the magistrate.
The officials explained that a move to prevent Ganjin from
leaving China had been instigated by the monk Ling-yu,
prominent among the disciples of Ganjin. Ling-yu, then in

residence at the Lung-hsing Monastery in Yang-chou, commanded great prestige in the region north of the Yangtze. He had enlisted the support of ranking clerics of various monasteries and petitioned the government to intervene. As a result, the magistrate of Chiang-tung Province* had sent warrants down to the *chou* offices, and senior monks of monasteries along Ganjin's route of travel were being arrested and interrogated in order to trace the whereabouts of the travelers. It was from concern for the safety of his teacher, Ganjin, that Ling-yu had opposed the venture from the very beginning.

The monks spent more than a dozen days in detention at the Ch'an-lin Monastery. The authorities at last decided to have them escorted overland back to Yang-chou, but the trip could not be made immediately. During their tedious sojourn at Ch'an-lin, Fushō unexpectedly encountered Kaiyū.

At the behest of a resident monk, Fushō walked out to the gate to meet with an anonymous Japanese monk; there stood Kaiyū, in the garb of a mendicant. Almost nine years had sped by since the spring of 736, when Kaiyū had left the Great Fu-hsien Monastery in Lo-yang. He had changed of course. His complexion was dusky, and his bulky frame had become soft and even bulkier with middle age. Kaiyū had come to Ch'an-lin-ssu from the opposite direction, from Fu-chou, and had been traveling toward T'ien-t'ai Mountain when he heard about Ganjin. Having learned that Japanese monks were in the group, he had come to the monastery to satisfy his curiosity.

"So it was you, after all," Kaiyū began in Chinese. But he changed immediately to Japanese. "What are you doing in this part of the country?" he asked. Fushō was momentarily overcome by nostalgia. Briefly he described what had happened since their parting at Lo-yang and told Kaiyū about the projected voyage and how the plans had been beset by a series of mishaps.

"The two of you have certainly had a difficult time, and I'm really sympathetic," Kaiyu said in earnest. And he added, as if amazed by their troubles, "Here you are, a jewel in the

*The area south of the lower reaches of the Yangtze.

palm of your hands, wandering about the coast in the vain hope of crossing over to those little islands beyond the sea. It's all so ironic."

Fushō asked Kaiyū what he had been doing. Kaiyū said he had not yet accomplished anything noteworthy and whatever was to be done still lay in the future. But he had traveled much since their last meeting. He had seen deserts, and he had seen an ocean full of serpentine creatures. There were yet many, many places he would like to visit.

Kaiyū suddenly steered the conversation onto another course. "I no longer care to return to Japan," he said.

"Do you mean to say you'll spend the rest of your life here?" Fushō asked.

"Most likely." Kaiyū's expression was serious. "I have no parents, no brothers or sisters. So why must I go back to Japan? I was born in Japan, but is that reason enough?"

Because Fushō did not answer, Kaiyū restated his point: "Must I go back to Japan simply because the blood coursing through my veins is Japanese blood?"

Again Fushō did not answer. He could not think of an appropriate answer to this question. He was hoping to return to Japan because he wanted to. He believed an individual's wish, not logic, determined his course of action.

Yōei had been summoned by officials for questioning. Although Fushō tried to detain Kaiyū until Yōei returned, Kaiyū said he had not particularly missed Yōei but would be pleased, nonetheless, to have his good wishes conveyed to him, and he left.

Intense nostalgia registered in Yōei's face when he was told that Kaiyū had been there, but it vanished in an instant. He spoke of Kaiyū with brooding anger: there was no real bond between Kaiyū and themselves; whatever seemed estimable to them was never so regarded by Kaiyū, whatever his reasons; Kaiyū was better off disregarding others and following a path of his own choosing.

When the monks were returned to Yang-chou, Ganjin was placed in the custody of the Lung-hsing Monastery, of which he was still the superior cleric. At this point the disintegration of the project was complete. Of the more than thirty that made up his own party, Ganjin urged all but his immediate disciples to return to their home provinces. He made arrangements for Fushō and Yōei to remain at the monastery until suitable quarters could be found for them.

When Ganjin's arrival became widely known, well-wishers from all walks of life came in a steady stream to the Lung-hsing Monastery, bringing with them words of felicitation for Ganjin and offerings for the altar. But Ganjin was cheerless and silent in the wake of his enforced return to Yang-chou, and seemed reluctant to meet with anyone. He was adamant in his refusal to see his disciple Ling-yu, who had turned informant, though with good intentions. Ling-yu, in a show of penance, remained standing from sundown to sunup for sixty nights, but Ganjin was unmoved. His ire subsided only when clerics from various monasteries took pity on Ling-yu and interceded on his behalf.

Hsiang-yen and Ssu-ch'a were visibly and understandably cheerful; they were back in the city they thought they had left forever, and were able to meet friends they had never expected to see again. The young Ssu-ch'a had not lost his zest for adventure, and continued to dream of a journey to Japan. Hsiang-yen, already past forty, would have willingly followed his teacher Ganjin anywhere, though he was not inclined to risk a hazardous voyage. The year of wandering had taken its toll of Hsiang-yen; his gentle face burned dark by the sun, his cheeks hollow, he could scarcely be recognized by those who had known him before.

Yōei was naturally more disheartened than the others. It was not so much the collapse of his plans that had driven him to despair as his loss of hope. Another voyage seemed out of the question. The magistrate of Huai-nan Province had charged the senior clerics of the Lung-hsing Monastery with the responsibility for preventing Ganjin from again setting sail for a foreign country. In these circumstances, Yōei could not prevail upon Ganjin to divulge his intention.

A seed of doubt had been planted in Fushō's mind. He wondered whether a monk so eminent as Ganjin should be exposed to such hardship and peril in order to be taken to Japan. He knew that he would eventually have to part with

Ganjin, and this weighed heavily on his mind. Fushō had spent a year of suffering and hardship with Ganjin, attending the venerable monk at all times, and he was saddened to think they would soon be separated, but he was aware that the government would not relax its surveillance over Ganjin so long as he and Yōei remained with him. Their presence only made matters more difficult for him. They would have to leave Yang-chou at the earliest opportunity.

Yōei and Fushō had been at the Lung-hsing Monastery three months when they decided to leave; they informed Ganjin of their decision. Ganjin pondered it awhile, then said to them, "It may be for the best. But come back whenever you wish. We are working on behalf of Buddha's Law, and I doubt whether there will be any wavering in my determination to sail for Japan."

After they parted from Ganjin, the two Japanese asked each other what he might have meant when he said to come back whenever they wished; they had no idea when they would return to Yang-chou. They concluded that they should probably wait until the incident was forgotten and the name of Ganjin no longer associated with Japan.

Later in the day Yōei and Fushō ventured outside the monastery for the first time since their return. They went to the Ch'an-chih Monastery to visit Gōgyō. Ch'an-chih was situated a mile beyond the rise surmounted by the Small City. Sparse groves of bare trees bordered the road; the winter sun shed its meager rays on the uninhabited low hills. At the monastery, they were told that Gōgyō had gone away two months before. No one knew his destination. He had left several boxes of texts he had transcribed for safekeeping at the monastery. The two monks surmised that whatever writings were contained in those few wooden boxes represented only a fraction of what Gōgyō had amassed, and that Gōgyō had probably divided his ponderous accumulation of scrolls for storage at several monasteries.

The next day Yōei and Fushō left the Lung-hsing Monastery. They were escorted by Hsiang-yen and Ssu-ch'a as far as Twin Bridge beyond the west wall of the city. There the two Japanese monks bade farewell to the two monks of China. It was then the end of February in 745.

9

In the spring of 748, Yōei and Fushō returned to Yang-chou from T'ung-an County (the vicinity of An-ch'ing in Anhwei Province) in order to talk with Ganjin. The two had spent three years in a provincial coastal town on the Yangtze, far from the metropolis, waiting for the furor over Ganjin's projected travel to subside and the incident to be forgotten. Yōei was now past his mid-forties, and Fushō not far behind in years.

During those three years in T'ung-an County, there was no single happening of such magnitude that the entire nation was aroused. On two or three occasions, barbarians were reported to have violated the border, but the news came months after the incidents. Peace continued to prevail over the great T'ang empire. The greatest stir occurred a year before when Emperor Hsüan-tsung raised the famed twenty-nine-year-old beauty, Yang T'ai-chen, to the position of imperial consort with the rank of *kuei-fei*.* The appointment of An Lu-shan, a special favorite of the emperor, as the ranking official at the imperial court caused momentary excitement, and also the news that Premier Li Lin-fu had been awarded tribute goods, which accumulated annually in the vaults. The arbitrary execution of state ministers was becoming a rather common occurrence. In 748, about the time the monks returned to Yang-chou, death sentences were meted out to Wei Chien and Li Shih-chih, both high officials. Though times were generally peaceful, the stage was being set for great turbulence to come.

Yōei and Fushō were once again able to stroll the city streets of Yang-chou. They went to Ch'ung-fu Monastery, where they had been told Ganjin was living. When the three were together again, Ganjin spoke to them in his usual serene manner.

"I am glad you came. It has been four years since our travels were interrupted. I believe this time, with the protection of the Buddha, we shall at long last realize our wish."

---

*She is the famous Yang Kuei-fei, who reigned supreme in the imperial menage but was put to death during the rebellion of the red-bearded general, An Lu-shan.

His voice was resonant, he seemed brimming with vigor. Although Ganjin was now sixty, he seemed more youthful than before.

Yōei and Fushō were to remain at Ch'ung-fu Monastery until summer in order to prepare secretly for another voyage. This time the ship would be built at the New Canal, and the monks would put together more or less what they had taken on board in 743. In ten days the list of voyagers was drawn up. The central group of fourteen would consist of Yōei, Fushō, Hsiang-yen, Shen-ts'ang, Kuang-yen, Tun-wu, Tao-tzu, Ju-kao, Te-ch'ing, Jih-wu, Ssu-ch'a, and several lay persons. In addition, there would be a crew of eighteen as well as thirty-five others who sought passage. Prodded by recollections of their previous misadventures, they worked rapidly.

Toward the end of May, when preparations for sailing were almost complete, Yōei reminded Fushō of the one task yet remaining: they must find Gōgyō and offer to take some of his transcribed texts as cargo. It would be foolhardy to risk carrying all that Gōgyō had accumulated. The sacred writings, Yōei suggested, should be divided into several items of cargo to be transported by different vessels; if Gōgyō consented, they would take part of the valuable cargo with them. Fushō concurred. They could not know whether Gōgyō might have some other scheme in mind. But then Gōgyō had entrusted his scrolls for safekeeping to several monasteries, ostensibly against total loss from fire or theft. An ocean crossing, with one's fate at the mercy of a whim of heaven, presented an even greater risk, and it would be foolish to consign all the texts to a single ship. Though he surely would have no such thought in mind, his permission would have to be obtained.

Fushō went to the Ch'an-chih Monastery that day and inquired about Gōgyō, but no one knew his whereabouts. He had left some of his scrolls in the custody of the monastery, but he had not been heard from in three years. His past gave no clue to where he might have gone. He could be in Lo-yang or possibly in Ch'ang-an.

There was nothing more Fushō could do. Having made inquiries at his only source of information, he abandoned the search. A few days afterward, however, a monk of Ta-ming-ssu told him that a Japanese Buddhist had come recently to the Indian Monastery. Fushō thought the Buddhist might well be Gōgyō and set off immediately to find out.

The Indian Monastery stood near Shan-kuang-ssu, just outside the city, in an area along the Grand Canal that contained numerous grave markers and many white-walled shrines dedicated to local gods. It was directly across Ch'an-chih-ssu on the opposite bank.

Fushō was led to a room on the side of the main hall; as he entered it, he caught sight of the back of a pitifully withered figure, hunched up against a desk. He had seen it many times before.

When Gōgyō turned his head to acknowledge his visitor, Fushō saw an unearthly countenance. He thought it streaked with blood. But he soon realized that the red and blue streaks about Gōgyō's lips were ink. The aged monk was using a painting brush. On a large sheet of paper spread out on his desk were depictions of several figures of the bodhisattva Avalokita in a pose of thoughtful meditation. The figures were crudely done, as if by a child, and the outlines filled in here and there with color.

"What are you painting?"

Fushō dispensed with the usual pleasantries and started the conversation in blunt fashion. Gōgyō did not give him a direct answer.

"Well . . ." he began slowly, "lately I've been copying texts that deal with the rituals of Esoteric Buddhism."

Indeed, there were drawings of all kinds scattered about the room. There were copies of mandalas as well as sketches of their details, sketches of right hands of bodhisattvas with various objects in their grasp, and depictions of diadems and oddly shaped flasks—all outlined and colored quite clumsily.

Gōgyō said that now that he had finished the task of transcribing texts translated into Chinese by I-Ching, he would devote his efforts wholly to reproducing works describing the rituals of Esoteric Buddhism. This would keep him busy until the day, years away perhaps, when ships of the next embassy came from Japan.

"It's turned out to be a much bigger job than the one before. There's no end to this one."

In the clutter about Gōgyō's desk, Fushō saw sutras, paintings of Buddhist images, and a great many unsuccessful attempts at sketching. He leafed through a book titled *Two-Part Sutra of the Infinite Birth* as he related the purpose of his visit. He worded his comments carefully so as not to alarm Gōgyō, but when he mentioned his wish to take some of Gōgyō's scrolls aboard their ship, the aged monk started.

"As you say," Gōgyō said finally, after a long silence, "they should probably be divided and transported aboard several ships. There's no reason for me to accompany them. All that matters is getting them to Japan. If you're certain they will be delivered, you may take them."

"I can't possibly make such a promise," Fushō replied. "But let me say this. Should the ship ever be in danger of foundering and the cargo have to be thrown overboard, I'll go into the sea in place of your scrolls."

Fushō, at that moment, was convinced of the truth of his words. He did not know whether the scrolls would reach Japan, but he thought he could carry out the promise he had made. The aged Japanese monk, whose lips were tinged with red and blue, exerted a power that compelled Fushō to think so, indeed say so.

Three days afterward, Gōgyō came to Ch'ung-fu Monastery with Chinese haulers bearing two heavy crates filled with transcribed Buddhist texts. That evening, Yōei, Fushō, and Gōgyō dined together. At one point, the conversation turned to Genrō, about whom Gōgyō had some recent news.

When Gōgyō was in Ch'ang-an the year before, he had come across Genrō and his Chinese wife and children. He and Genrō had stood at a street corner in the commercial section of the capital and chatted, but only briefly. He did not ask Genrō where he was living or what he was doing. The fact that he was dressed in a Buddhist robe suggested that he still belonged to the clergy. That was all Gōgyō could tell them. Others would have managed to learn considerably more, but this information was as much as anyone could expect from Gōgyō.

When he hobbled off toward the Indian Monastery, which was a good mile away, the old monk's face was flushed from the little wine he had sipped. As Fushō escorted him to the gate, he noted that Gōgyō's back was so bent that he seemed every bit a cripple.

Preparations for the voyage were completed in early June. Yōei, in consultation with Ganjin, selected the twenty-seventh of the month as the day for boarding. In order to avert disclosure of their plan, the monks divided themselves into small groups that day and proceeded separately to the embarkation point on the New Canal.

Gales swept over the region south of the Yangtze during the middle of the month, but fair weather prevailed after the twentieth. Ganjin left Ch'ung-fu Monastery at dusk on the appointed day, accompanied by Hsiang-yen and Ssu-ch'a. Just outside the south gate of the walled city they were joined by Yōei and Fushō, who had set out earlier. The five monks walked along the canal, which coursed from the city to the Yangtze River, stopped at a confluence of the canal with a tributary, and concealed themselves amidst reeds. At a pre-determined hour they proceeded to the embarking area, which was not far away. More than sixty men were already on board the ship.

It was on a moonlit night in 743 that the party had pre-viously set sail, but this one was pitch dark. The vessel was slightly smaller than the one that had carried them before, and less than half the size of those that had brought the em-bassy from Japan in 733. The passengers, sprawled out on the deck planks, were sheltered by a simple overhead cover instead of the customary gabled superstructure.

The ship sailed past the settlement of Kua-chou on the New Canal and into the flow of the Yangtze, then eastward down the great river to Lang-shan. Because the wind was rising, the crew kept the vessel on a course that circled the three islands in midstream. By daybreak the wind had sub-sided. The voyagers resumed their descent of the Yangtze to the estuary and touched at tiny San-t'a Island, in the jurisdic-tional zone of Yüeh-chou, where they would lie at anchor until favorable winds prevailed. They were there a month before they could sail with the wind again. When they reached Shu-feng Island, they lay in wait for another thirty days. Already it was October.

At daybreak on the sixteenth, Ganjin described a dream: "Last night I dreamt I saw three officials. One was dressed in a scarlet robe, and the other two wore robes of green. The three men waved to us from the shore. It occurs to me that the gods of China may have come to bid us farewell. I feel that we shall make the crossing safely this time." Only Hsiang-yen and Fushō were awake to hear Ganjin speak.

Soon the air began to stir. The wind had been blowing against them since the beginning of the month, but now it was blowing directly north. Surely a wind sent by the gods who appeared in Ganjin's dream, Hsiang-yen and Fushō thought. The crew was ready to sail.

Early the next morning the anchor was lifted, the ship left the shore of Shu-feng, and headed toward Ting-han Island. During the morning a small island was sighted on the southeast horizon. It might have been Ting-han. By midday it had disappeared from view. Everyone now marvelled at the fullness of the open sea. At dusk the winds gathered force, raising towering waves. The waters in which they sailed were now an eerie ink-black. During the night the winds gathered even greater force and turned the ship into a chip of wood, a plaything of the waves. Again and again the vessel carrying the seventy men would be sent plunging from the tops of mountainous crests down into the hollows of the waves, and once more up to the foaming crests.

As the voyagers intoned the *Sutra of the Bodhisattva Avalokita*, they heard the shouts of the shipmaster over the din of the storm.

"She'll go down unless we do something! Throw everything over the side! Now!"

The shipmaster felt compelled to act. He fought to reach the base of the mast, where he placed his hands on the cargo. Several of the crew rushed to help him.

Fushō, sitting beside the two crates of scrolls entrusted to him by Gōgyō, told himself he mustn't let them be jettisoned. A large garu-wood basket lay on top of the crates. Apparently intent on starting with the heaviest, the shipmaster shoved Fushō aside and wrestled with the crates, but could not so much as budge them. He picked up the garu-wood basket instead.

A sudden lurch sent several seamen sprawling. The ship-master, basket and all, fell over Fushō, then with a wild shout, sprang to his feet. His right leg was caught between Fushō and a crewman. Fushō held fast to the leg despite the torrent of seawater that poured in on him.

"Thou shalt not!"

A voice rang out of the angry darkness above them. The startled man dropped the basket.

"Thou shalt not!"

Again the voice rang out, and the shipmaster staggered and fell backward as if struck by an unseen force. He was not the only one who had heard the voice, and they all talked about it afterward. Ssu-ch'a and Yōei had heard it distinctly; Hsiang-yen said he thought he had heard a voice, although the words were indistinct. Fushō's frantic efforts had pre-vented his taking notice of anything else.

The tempest continued unabated into the evening. That night another miracle occurred while all hands were battling the wind and the seawater that invaded the hold. The ship-master's voice was heard again in fragments over the din of the storm.

"There's nothing more to fear! Look, everyone! Look at the god clad in armor and holding a scepter! He's standing at the prow! And another, at the foot of the mast!"

Everyone's glance went to the prow, and then to the mast. There was only darkness. But the shipmaster's words were reassuring, and the terror welling within them became less forbidding.

The storm winds eased somewhat the next day; but the ship, still tossed by ponderous waves, was being carried by a swift current in an unknown direction. Members of the crew seemed to think that the direction of their drift was away from Japan. Whether they would reach Japan was no longer anyone's concern. They would have touched land anywhere to be able to stand again on firm ground.

On the third day the ship sailed into snake-infested waters. The surface of the sea was alive with serpentine creatures measuring between five and ten feet in length, some even longer. Fūshō recalled that Kaiyū had told him four years before, when they had last met at Ch'an-lin Monastery, of having seen a sea of snakes; Kaiyū must have sailed in the same waters.

After three days they left the sea of snakes, and sailed for another three days in the zone of flying fish. Approximately a foot in length, these fish became flashes of silvery whiteness the instant they broke the surface, and the air before the ship was filled with a strange light. Then for five days the passengers saw flocks of large birds migrating across the waters. The birds occasionally swarmed down onto the ship to rest their wings, and each time the vessel groaned under their weight. When the men tried to scare them away, the birds attacked, tearing at them with their sharp beaks.

For two days following, the wind blew steadily, and the vessel continued to drift with the current. Everyone lay prostrate on the deck. Fushō alone retained his vigor; he went about the ship distributing grains of rice daily. Although Ssu-ch'a lay helpless on the deck throughout the day, occasionally he would turn over to jot down his thoughts, scribbling them in tiny letters on the reverse sides of scrolls. Yōei, never a good voyager, lay still, as though lifeless. Seasickness and disappointment over yet another failure had so exhausted his strength that he could not speak. How often, Fushō thought, had he seen Yōei like this?

They were tortured most by thirst. Their parched throats would not permit the ingestion of rice particles, nor could the gritty substance be ejected from their mouths; their stomachs would become bloated the instant they drank from the sea. Never before, they told one another, had they been subjected to such torture.

One day the voyagers saw several golden fish, each more than ten feet long. Hsiang-yen was the first to see them. The fish stayed with the ship, swimming round and round it. The day after, the wind lost its force, and an island came into view in the distance.

When the wind had slackened and the sea was again calm, Ganjin arose, walked to the prow of the ship, and sat down facing the waters ahead. The other monks also arose and took their places behind him. Fushō studied Ganjin's face and his eyes, fixed on the far horizon, and saw in them an inviolable dignity. Ganjin seemed not much different from usual, except that he had fallen silent.

Shortly before noon, Yōei, who was seated immediately behind Ganjin, broke the silence. "I just now dreamed that a government official came to me and asked that I administer the Buddhist vows to him. When I told him of my thirst and asked for water, he promptly gave me a liquid the color of milk, with an indescribably exquisite taste. I told him that there were seventy others aboard this ship who were as thirsty as I, and asked for more water—whereupon he summoned forth the old man who controls the rain and gave this command: 'You should be able to manage this easily. Quickly! Give water to those men on the ship.' And then my dream was broken. I am certain it will rain."

The men pinned their hopes on this augury. In midafternoon of the following day, water-laden clouds appeared from the southwest and filled the skies; in great drops the rain began to fall. Was this, in truth, a fulfillment of Yōei's dream? They wondered. For a short time the rain bore down on them in sheets while everyone stood on deck, catching the water in bowls. Again, the next day, the rains came, fully slaking their thirst.

On the day following the rains, the men found themselves fast approaching an island. Four white fish were sighted swimming before the ship as if to guide it. They soon found entrance into a protected bay. There the voyagers scaled precipitous cliffs to search for water. Once on the island they crossed a rise that was overspread with a dense growth of trees bearing giant leaves such as they had never seen before, and beyond it they saw a pond of clear water. They drank their fill and then carried back a supply of water to the ship.

They decided to lie at anchor for a time. After several days the men set out for the rise again to fetch water, but the pond was no longer there. "It must have been put there by a divine spirit," they told one another, and Hsiang-yen and Ssu-ch'a seemed to believe this. But Fushō thought it had most likely been trapped rain water that was quickly absorbed by the porous soil.

It was already November. Though it should have been cold, there were no signs of winter. The trees bore exotic fruits, flowers were in bloom, and bamboo sprouted from the earth. All was typical of summer.

After remaining at anchor off shore for a fortnight, they found a cove where the ship could be moored; all hands were then able to go ashore. The voyagers formed parties to search for settlements of local inhabitants. Fortunately they soon encountered a party of four Chinese, who urged them to leave the island at once lest they fall victims to the natives, who trapped and feasted on human beings.

The men rushed back to their ship and took it into a different cove, one that seemed to offer them safety. But that night, aborigines, armed with swords, found their way to the vessel. When they were given food, they retreated quietly, but the voyagers were terrified and put out to sea though it was dark, setting their course for the island of Hainan, which the Chinese had described to them earlier that day. Three days later they sailed into an estuary in Chen-chou, on the southern tip of Hainan Island.

The morning was spent unloading the cargo. Three crewmen carried the boxes containing Gōgyō's scrolls onto the white sand under the glare of the sun. One of the men irreverently sat on the boxes while he quenched his thirst. In the afternoon everyone submitted to questioning by local officials. The voyagers spent the entire day on the sandy beach, then posted a guard to watch the cargo and went back to the ship for the night.

Because neither Yōei nor Fushō had any clear notion of geography, they could not envision a route back to Japan. They were aware only of being at the mouth of a river at the southern tip of an island that was situated south of the southernmost boundary of the vast continental expanse of the T'ang empire.

Ganjin was reserved and silent, as he had been before when his efforts came to naught. His face reflected nothing of his thoughts or emotions. Hsiang-yen and Ssu-ch'a patterned their behavior on Ganjin's and maintained a guarded silence. Never before had those two failed to come to the two Japanese with consoling words when plans went awry and to reassure them that another opportunity would surely come. But this time was different. They showed no bitterness over having been made castaways in a remote land, nor did they express any disillusionment over yet another failure. Since neither Hsiang-yen nor Ssu-ch's, to speak the truth, were able to fathom Ganjin's thoughts, they maintained this pose lest they betray an attitude that might contradict his.

The coolness of the other monks toward Yōei and Fushō was obvious. They had been forced to look death in the eye time and again for the sake of the two Japanese. Why was this always their lot? They made no effort to mask their resentment.

For two or three days after the landing, everyone experienced a lethargy of the sort that affects men who have been long adrift at sea. On the fourth day, the deputy *chou* governor, Feng Ch'ung-ch'ai, accompanied by four hundred soldiers, came to investigate the report of their landing. He escorted the voyagers to the city of Chen-chou, a city unlike any they had ever seen. Shops, dwellings, and offices were low-roofed and sturdy to bear up against the tropical typhoon. Luxuriant southern vegetation of many exotic varieties surrounded the houses. The atmosphere was dry. One perspired in the sun, yet found coolness in the shade beneath trees.

Feng Ch'ung-ch'ai met with them in the stone-paved garden of a modest office structure and told them what he had dreamt the night before. He encountered a man who claimed to have been his father-in-law in a previous existence, and the man told him that he had been reborn and his soul now occupied the person of a monk by the name of Feng-t'ien. Surely the dream was an augury of an impending visit by his father-in-law of a prior existence. And he asked whether a monk named Feng-t'ien might be a member of their party. Hsiang-yen answered in behalf of Ganjin and expressed his regret, for there was no one by that name among them.

"Perhaps then," Feng Ch'ung-ch'ai said, "it was Ganjin of whom he spoke." The monks were invited into the office structure, and there they conducted services at an altar that had been erected for the occasion.

Feng's office served as their quarters for three days. Later, they were asked to perform Buddhist rites at the office of the governor, and there Ganjin administered the Buddhist vows to many government officials.

In due course, the monastery of Ta-yün was formally designated as quarters for Ganjin and some thirty others. In the eyes of those accustomed to the great Buddhist centers on the continent, the buildings as well as the monastery grounds appeared woefully derelict. The Hall of Buddha, in particular, was in total disrepair and on the verge of collapsing.

The travelers welcomed the new year of 748 in the dilapidated temple. There was no rain at all around that time. Every strong gust raised the powdery sand off the desert floor, and a fine dust would descend in a mist onto the crowded, squat houses of the tiny city. Ganjin and others rallied together the craftsmen of the area and initiated the construction of a new Hall of Buddha. The project, begun in the dry winter season, continued into the rainy season of summer. Having seen the construction through to its completion, the party of monks decided to set out for Wanan-chou on the southeast corner of the island, whence they could sail back to the mainland. Feng Ch'ung-ch'ai, the deputy governor, would escort them with eight hundred armed men.

On their departure, Ganjin presented the Ta-yün Monastery with the statuary, ceremonial equipment, and sutras that they were to have taken with them to Japan. Yōei and Fushō decided to make an offering of the two crates of texts, which Gōgyō had entrusted to their care. This seemed sensible in view of the long journey ahead of them, and they felt certain that Gōgyō would have done the same.

With the help of natives, they hauled the two heavy boxes to the new Hall of Buddha, which had been born of their efforts. During a walk of nearly a mile back to their lodging, Yōei needed to stop several times in order to rest in the shade of the palms. Fushō was concerned that Yōei might not be able to endure the long trek to Wanan-chou. Yōei had been greatly enfeebled during their sojourn in an unaccustomed tropical land, following on a harrowing voyage. Earlier, in 742, when they had first talked about returning to Japan, Fushō had been sickly, much as Yōei was now. Lacking confidence in his ability to endure, he had forsaken his plans to remain in China and further his studies. Seven years later, however, he was the hardy one, having been strengthened by continuing hardships in unaccustomed lands, and Yōei, who had been sturdy, was so debilitated that he turned feverish at the slightest exertion. An overland journey of more than forty days to Wanan-chou would be too taxing for Yōei. This was apparent to the others, and Ganjin arranged for Yōei to sail directly to the port of departure in Ai-chou. Fushō was to accompany him.

The two Japanese monks found passage on a vessel that left Chen-chou a few days after Ganjin and the others had set out. The sailing to Wanan-chou and then to Ai-chou required forty days.

In Ai-chou, the largest city on the island of Hainan, Fushō and Yōei hoped they could again enjoy the atmosphere of a metropolis. They found lodgings in an old Indian temple and awaited there the arrival of Ganjin's party. Yōei, now wretchedly thin, took to a sickbed immediately. Fushō, when he was not nursing Yōei, took every opportunity to stroll about the city. He saw a great many shops selling betel nuts, lichees, longans, bananas, and other exotic fruits called *i-chih, chü-en,* and *lou-t'ou.* Some were as large as platters and the nectar of all tasted sweeter than honey. Blooming everywhere in profusion were vivid flowers—mostly in brilliant reds, blues, and yellows.

Ganjin's party arrived in Ai-chou two weeks later than expected. The monks were welcomed into the city with great ceremony by the territorial marshal, Chang Yün, and then taken to K'ai-yüan Monastery. They had been escorted by Feng Ch'ung-ch'ai as far as the boundary of Ai-chou.

Fushō and Yōei, now reunited with the others, were told of their experiences en route. Some forty days after their departure from Chen-chou, Ganjin and his party arrived at Wanan-chou, where they were received by the great native chieftain, Feng Jo-fang, and entertained for three days at his residence. What they saw of Feng Jo-fang's mode of living they could scarcely believe. Whenever Feng entertained guests, he used frankincense merely to give light, burning more than one hundred pounds of the precious wood during an evening. They learned afterward that Feng Jo-fang's trade was the pirating of Persian argosies that sailed near the coast each year; he plundered the valuables and carried off the voyagers as slaves. In the garden behind his house, aromatic woods of various hues—red, black, purple, and white—rose in mountainous heaps, and precious booty of all kinds was in every open space of the house. His slaves lived in settlements; the monks were told that all villages within three days' travel north and south and five days' travel east and west were settlements of captive foreigners.

During their stay in Ai-chou, Fushō was often accompanied by Ssu-ch'a in his walks through the city. The men and women who crowded the streets of this city were excitingly strange in appearance. The men, wearing flat wooden hats, and the women, whose dress recalled the women of Japan, wore ornaments around their ankles, stained their teeth black, tattooed their faces, and took water through their nostrils.

Outside the city stood a grove of aromatic *tan-t'ang* trees. Whenever the wind stirred, the monks were told, the fragrance wafted over a distance of three miles. There was also a grove of Benares trees. Ssu-ch'a's notes provide this description of the tree: "The fruit is the size of a winter melon. The tree resembles the Chinese quince, its leaves are like those of the bulrush, and its root has the flavor of dried persimmon."

In this region, fields were planted in October, and the millet harvested in January. Sericulture flourished; there were eight crops of cocoons each year. Rice was harvested twice a year.

Marshal Chang Yün and his subordinates, in turn, called on the visitors. Once, Chang Yün himself supervised the preparation of a meal consisting of the fruit of the *yu-t'an-po-hua* and a delicacy made of the leaves of the tree.

"This is the fruit of the *yu-t'an-po-hua*," the marshal explained to Ganjin. "It is remarkable that the tree bears fruit, though there are never blossoms. It is indeed an extraordinary tree. That fate should have enabled us to meet seems no less remarkable."

Ssu-ch'a, who sat beside them, promptly sketched the *yu-t'an-po-hua* tree and recorded this description: "Its leaves are red, circular in shape, and measure a foot across. The sweet dark-purple fruit is delicious."

On their third day at the K'ai-yüan-ssu, a great conflagration raged through the city and destroyed the monastery. At the request of Marshal Chang Yün, Ganjin oversaw the reconstruction. Everyone except Yōei, who lay ill, was caught up in this activity. A complement of religious edifices had to be built, which would include, among others, the Hall of Buddha, a lecture hall, and a pagoda. The builders were immediately beset by the problem of acquiring the necessary lumber.

But Feng Ch'ung-ch'ai had learned of their problem and had sent slaves, each bearing a length of lumber, to Ai-chou. In three days the necessary material was assembled.

The monastery was completed earlier than scheduled and with wood that was left over Ganjin had sculptors fashion an image of Śākya Buddha ten feet tall. When all was finished, Ganjin mounted the dais to administer monastic vows, lecture on the *Vinaya,* and confer the priesthood on novices. It had been a long while since Fushō had observed the venerable monk in a pose of solemn ceremonial dignity, and he could not stem the flow of tears that coursed down his cheeks. Impaired in no way by long years of wandering, erecting temples, administering vows, and conferring the priesthood wherever he went, the venerable monk seemed to be the Buddha reincarnate.

Yōei compelled himself that day to leave his sick bed in order to attend the ceremony. After the ordination rituals, when all the monks had left the hall, he sought out Fushō.

"As I left the hall just now, for an instant I felt as if I were in a large monastery in Nara, back in our capital in Japan. With the color of the sky, the trees, and the earth so different, how could I have been deluded even momentarily into thinking we were back in Nara?" With some fervor he added that they must make certain of Ganjin's getting to Japan.

Many years earlier, having just been consulted by Ryūson

about coming to China, Yōei and Fushō had stood on the grounds of the Kōfuku-ji, basking in the sunlight of early spring and talking of the future. Fushō recalled that scene, for there they stood, as they had then, face to face, Yōei gazing down at him and Fushō looking up to his taller companion.

Gaunt and enfeebled, Yōei bore little resemblance to the man Fushō had first met at the Kōfuku-ji; only his unbending resolve had not left him. Fushō continued to gaze into the face of his friend. He was tempted to divulge the thoughts coursing through his mind, to tell Yōei that they ought then and there to make an end of this venture, the culmination of which would be Ganjin's presence in Japan as the transmitter of the codes of monasticism. Ganjin was old, and, besides, Yōei in his condition of debility could not possibly see the task through to its fulfillment.

Ganjin kept his thoughts wholly to himself, and said nothing about prospects of sailing for Japan. But his random comments indicated that he had no intention of returning to his home, Yang-chou. A decision would be made as soon as the monks reached Lei-chou on the opposite coast. Barring the unforeseen, Ganjin would very likely lead them straight to a convenient port of embarkation to Japan. Fushō was convinced, however, of the necessity to place Ganjin and Yōei in the protective custody of the government and to terminate this odyssey as quickly as possible.

As Fushō turned his gaze away from Yōei, he found himself able to resist the urge to speak out. He was aware that Yōei would turn a deaf ear on his suggestion and that such words would bring only cruel disappointment to his ailing companion.

Not long after, Ganjin announced his decision to leave Ai-chou. Marshal Chang Yün, grieved at parting with Ganjin, escorted the party beyond the city walls, and ordered the officials at the port of Teng-mai to escort the monks to the ship. It was more than a year after they had touched land at Chen-chou that the monks left Hainan Island and found themselves once again at sea. A voyage of two days and three nights brought them to Lei-chou.

10

Ganjin and his party again set foot on the continent. From Lei-chou, they traveled north through Lo-chou, Pien-chou, Hsiang-chou, Po-chou, and Hsiu-chou; then following the West River through Teng-chou to Wu-chou, thence by boat up the Cassia River, they came to Kuei-lin,* the administrative seat of Shih-an County. At each settlement they received a spirited welcome from officials, the clergy, and the townspeople. They planned to sail from Kuei-lin down the Hsiang River to the south basin of the Yangtze. That route of travel was not one that would lead to Japan. Had they gone to Canton, they might have found a ship bound for Japan, but Ganjin elected to forgo that possible opportunity. Yōei was disheartened to see his objective recede yet further into the future, but Fushō persuaded him of the wisdom of abiding by Ganjin's decision.

In Kuei-lin, the monks were out of the tropical zone and could enjoy an increased awareness of having come back to China. The color of the sky, the tint of the waters, and the rays of the sun were softly diffuse, neither strong nor brilliant, and the months were in agreement with the changing seasons.

The monks had not intended to remain long in Kuei-lin, but circumstances dictated a prolonged stay. Feng Ku-p'o, marshal of the county, had been informed of Ganjin's impending arrival. He betook himself on foot to a place outside the city walls, and as the venerable monk approched, he made deep obeisance. He then led the party to the local K'ai-yüan Monastery.

The doors of the Hall of Buddha, which had been sealed tightly for many years, were opened in honor of the occasion, and in moments the fragrance sealed within pervaded the atmosphere of the city. The clerics of Kuei-lin converged on the monastery, carrying banners, burning incense, and chanting hymns. The grounds were crowded with people from every walk of life who streamed in continually, day and night.

*A city situated some two hundred miles inland, northwest of Canton.

Marshal Feng Ku-p'o himself prepared meals for the monks. Soon he took the Vow of Bodhisattvas under Ganjin's ministration. Public officials and scholarly candidates for officialdom from the seventy-four *chou* in the province converged on the city and emulated the marshal by having the vow administered to them.

The monastery where the Buddhists were lodged was built during the Sui Dynasty* and was known initially as Yüan-hua-ssu. Once destroyed by fire, it was subsequently rebuilt, and designated one of the K'ai-yüan monasteries during the reign of Hsüan-tsung. The monks had been in Kuei-lin almost a year—much longer than they had intended to stay. Yōei's apparent recovery from his malady may have been due to the benign climate.

When they were about to terminate this sojourn, a petition for Ganjin to visit Canton was delivered by an emissary of Lu Huan, governor of Kuang-chou. Lu occupied several important offices, including that of Great Marshal of the South Sea Region. Although a journey to Canton meant traveling in a direction away from the Yangtze basin, Ganjin agreed to Lu Huan's request. Some of the monks were disgruntled by the prospect of straying so far from their intended route of travel; but Ganjin was firm in his decision, and they would abide by it.

Lu Huan, of the famous Lu clan of Fan-yang, was renowned for his intelligence and honesty and was held in deep trust by Emperor Hsüan-tsung. Yōei and Fushō had met this man more than ten years before, during their journey from Lo-yang to Ch'ang-an. Lu at that time was the magistrate of Shan-chou, and Emperor Hsüan-tsung, with whose entourage they were traveling, had stopped at Shan-chou in order to acclaim his administration and inscribe a poem of praise on the wall of his office. The two Japanese monks remembered him well, but Lu could not have been expected to remember them.

All municipalities lining the route to Canton were notified by Lu Huan of Ganjin's impending visit; they were to extend appropriate courtesies to the travelers. When the monks were leaving Kuei-lin, Marshal Feng Ku-p'o took Ganjin's hand

*The dynasty, dating 589–618, that immediately preceded the T'ang.

to lead him to the ship; he spoke these words of parting: "The time has finally come for us to part, and we may not meet again during this existence. May we meet in the celestial palace of the bodhisattva Maitreya."* The monks, too, grieved over their parting with the people of Kuei-lin, who had been charitable hosts for a year. Yōei's health was again failing, and he was wracked by high fever. Fushō, Ssu-ch'a, and Hsiang-yen carried Yōei's inflamed body onto the ship after everyone else had gone aboard.

"A sailing of seven days down the Cassia River brought us to Wu-chou. Then we proceeded to the Lung-hsing Monastery in Tuan-chou. The monk Yōei died quite suddenly. It was a pity to see Ganjin so possessed with grief. Having observed mourning, we made our departure." This is the only reference to Yōei's death, in the *Record of the Eastward Journey of the Great Monk of T'ang*. The author of the *Record*, to whom Ssu-ch'a made his journal available, may in this instance have quoted Ssu-ch'a faithfully.

Because Yōei's illness had suddenly become critical, the party of Buddhists, having sailed down the Cassia River to Wu-chou and from there into the main stream, broke their journey at Tuan-chou, midway in their cruise down the West River. They went directly to the Lung-hsing Monastery. By the time they were being escorted by local officials through the main gate of the monastery, Yōei was already enveloped by the shadow of death.

Sitting at the pillowside of Yōei's lifeless body, Ganjin spoke to him as if he were still alive: "Because of my concern for your health, beloved Yōei, I had selected a route that would take us through Kuei-lin to the Yangtze, for that would have taken us out of the torrid region. I acceded to the request to visit Kuang-chou only because you seemed to have regained strength. Rather than return to the Yangtze region, I thought we might proceed to Canton and seek passage to Japan. To think it has all been in vain!" As Ganjin's words trailed off, the sobbing of the monks became audible.

On the following day, Yōei was buried in the high ground

*Maitreya, designated the future world-savior, is said to dwell within a bejeweled palace in a Buddhist realm high atop mythical Mount Sumeru.

behind the Lung-hsing Monastery. Fushō scattered a handful of earth over Yōei's remains, and Ganjin, Hsiang-yen, and Ssu-ch'a each did the same. The year 749 was drawing to a close; sixteen years had gone by since the Japanese monks arrived in China in 733.

Fushō was now the only Japanese among them. Some of the monks had never truly countenanced Ganjin's plan; it was Yōei who had kept them inspired. His zeal had touched Ganjin, and, since 742, it had kept the party together in pursuit of a wholly unpredictable venture. Fushō, too, could not have endured eight years of arduous wandering without constant encouragement from Yōei. Whenever the group's efforts were balked and doubt arose in his mind, always it was Yōei's indomitable will that had prevailed. Now he would no longer be with them.

Having observed mourning, the monks left the Lung-hsing Monastery. They were escorted by the governor of Tuan-chou to their destination. At Canton they were welcomed by Governor Lu Huan and a host of people who had come to the outskirts of the city to meet them; they were received with elaborate ceremony, and then led to the Ta-yün-ssu. On the grounds of the monastery stood a pair of myrobalan trees bearing fruit that resembled the giant jujube. Amid these hospitable surroundings, they mounted the ordination platform and administered monastic vows.

Fushō, lest he dwell in melancholy over Yōei's death, strolled through the city daily, visiting the famed scenic sites and Buddhist temples. Canton, a city encircled by three walls, was ruled by Lu Huan, who held firm control over the civil as well as the military and whose prestige rivaled that of Emperor Hsüan-tsung. The city was crowded; even the outskirts were packed tightly with shops and houses. As Fushō looked out far beyond the city walls he beheld a scene of haunting beauty. Forests of lichee trees stretched for miles, and the red fruit was like scattered jewels in the lush green. It was rumored in the streets of Canton at the time that Emperor Hsüan-tsung had recently had the fragrant ambrosial fruit carried by swift horsemen to Ch'ang-an as a gift for his beloved consort, Yang Kuei-fei.

Fushō visited the K'ai-yüan Monastery of Canton and saw the fabled sandalwood tablet depicting the teachings of the *Avataṁsaka Sūtra*. The tablet was the product of thirty years' work by sixty artisans, the cost of three hundred thousand strings of cash having been borne by a foreigner who had resided at the monastery. It was to have been taken to India, but when the magistrate Liu Chu-lin brought this plan to the attention of the government, the Emperor decreed its retention in the monastery. The tablet was embellished with precious gems, and its beauty defied description.

Fushō also visited the three Brahman monasteries where Indian monks were in residence. On the grounds of one was a pond, its surface carpeted with a species of green lotus that Ssu-ch'a described thus in his notes: "The blossoms, leaves, root, stalk, and fragrance—all are wondrously exotic."

While he was at the monastery with the lotus-covered pond, Fushō was told that a monk from Japan had been living there for the past six months. He longed desperately to see a countryman and returned to the monastery time and again, but the monk was never present. About a month had gone by when, on yet another visit, he peered into the structure that stood beside a small and colorful sequestered gate and discovered to his surprise that the monk within was Kaiyū. The two looked into each other's eyes in disbelief, and then clasped each other's arms. Kaiyū had been unable to weather the onslaught of years and showed unmistakable signs of aging. The bizarreness of his grin was due to gaps left by missing teeth. He said he had known that Ganjin and Fushō were in the city, and when Fushō took him to task for not having come to see them, Kaiyū replied in his old cynical manner.

"I've come to detest encounters with Japanese. When a person has made up his mind never again to set foot in his homeland, he's repelled by anything that reeks of his homeland."

Perhaps because he had been living with Brahman monks, Kaiyū seemed to have acquired the traits of his companions. His body was now lean and dark, but well padded with clothing as only an Indian monk's would be. When Fushō informed him of Yōei's death, Kaiyū's face took on a somber cast. "Yōei's death is a great loss," he said, and closed his eyes in silent prayer.

Later in the day Kaiyū led Fushō down to the harbor to dine on unusual foreign fare. The port at the mouth of the Red River was teeming with ships from India, Malaya, and Persia. The vessels, masts soaring sixty to seventy feet above the water, were laden with cargo from lands far away. Fushō saw men whose skin and eyes were shades quite different from his. He had heard before about these men—from the Lion Country, the Country of Great Rocks, the Ku-t'ang Nation, the land of white barbarians, land of red barbarians*—but had never before seen them. Most of them were said to be living aboard their ships.

Rows of tightly wedged restaurants bordered congested streets near the pier. As they drank strange wines in one of them, Kaiyū told Fushō of his desire to travel to India. He would go by ship and then return overland to China by the route described by the monk Hsüan-tsang in his *Record of the Regions West of the Great T'ang Empire*. Kaiyū mentioned several routes to India which Hsüan-tsang and other Chinese Buddhists had taken, and he talked of chronicles in which those routes were described. But Fushō recognized none of the names, for he knew little about such writings.

"Getting across an ocean has been a problem for both of us," Kaiyū said airily.

True, this problem had weighed heavily on them both. Yet he and Kaiyū had different purposes, and Fushō was tempted to remind Kaiyū of the deeper significance of his own endeavor. But he refrained from protesting what he considered objectionable levity in Kaiyū's remark; nor did he denigrate Kaiyū's aspirations. They were, after all, two Japanese, quite alone at a port crowded with foreigners, listening to alien speech, and gazing at ships from remote lands.

That night Fushō learned much about Gōgyō. Although Kaiyū seemed unmoved by Fushō's recounting of the adversities he and Yōei had met with over the years, when the

*The Lion Country is Ceylon, and the Country of Great Rocks is the Arabian Peninsula. The others have not been identified.

conversation turned to Gōgyō, he found someone worthy of extravagant praise. Yet, Kaiyū had not once seen the aging monk. Information concerning Gōgyō evidently reached him through his own private way of gleaning news, and he had much to tell. Gōgyō was at the Great Fu-shien Monastery in Lo-yang, still occupied with the task of transcribing texts on the rituals of Esoteric Buddhism. He was the recipient of unusual courtesies, and was being provided with lodging as well as clothing and food. But he was a shadow of his former self, his body having shrunk even more, his back bent still further, and his vision failing. It was an image familiar to Fushō.

Fushō saw Kaiyū only once. When he went again to the Brahman Monastery, he learned that Kaiyū had left for an unknown destination in the company of a host of Indian monks.

Ganjin and his party spent the spring in Canton. Though the port was frequented by ships that plied the sea routes to foreign lands, there were none bound for Japan. Ganjin ultimately abandoned his plan to seek passage to Japan in Canton, and decided instead to set out first for Shao-chou, and travel on to the south Yangtze region. When the monks departed, people of Canton escorted them far beyond the boundary of the city.

They sailed more than two hundred miles up the North River to reach Shao-chou. They slept soundly that night, at the Ch'an-chü Monastery, at last on firm ground. In the morning they were greeted by officials and residents of Shao-chou and given lodging in the Fa-ch'üan Monastery in the outskirts of the city. Fa-ch'üan had been built by the former Empress Wu for the Zen teacher Hui-neng. Hui-neng had been dead thirty-eight years, but his likeness was preserved in the room he had occupied. The monks stayed there but briefly, and then moved to the K'ai-yüan Monastery.

By then Fushō had decided what course he would take. He knew he could not replace Yōei as the one to spur Ganjin and the other monks on to new adventures. Besides, having forefeited his privileges as a student-monk from Japan, he no longer had official status. He could not foretell what harsh treatment he would receive at the hands of government officials once he set foot in Yang-chou, for he would certainly be regarded as the instigator of the enterprise to take Ganjin away from China. The status of the lone Japanese monk among them seemed indeed precarious, and Hsiang-yen and Ssu-ch'a said as much.

"Ever since Yōei died," Hsiang-yen told Fushō, "Ganjin hasn't spoken at all about Japan. We haven't been able to fathom his intention. We don't know whether he still contemplates going to Japan or whether he's given up the idea altogether. Nevertheless, his will shall be ours. If he embarks on another voyage for Japan, we'll accompany him. But if he abandons the idea and decides to remain in China, we'll stay here with him."

"Our course is clear," he added. "But your predicament is unlike ours. You have to return to Japan regardless of what Ganjin may decide to do."

Ssu-ch'a said nothing, but it was apparent that the young monk was in full accord with Hsiang-yen. As for the others in the party, it was obvious—though no one said so—that, since Yōei's death, they were against going to Japan.

Only Ganjin's thoughts remained unknown to Fushō. Ganjin spoke not a word about prospects of sailing for Japan. And his face, though as ever expressive of purpose and resolution, gave no clue to what coursed through his mind. His immediate destination was Yang-chou, and this was all that could be known.

Fushō knew that if he were to separate himself from the party, despite what Ganjin may have in mind, the project, which had been binding on them all, would be dissolved, Most of the monks would welcome this, and neither Hsiang-yen nor Ssu-ch'a would necessarily be disappointed. It was a matter of great importance to Japan that Ganjin be taken there in order to institute orthodox monasticism. Who could decide, though, whether so exalted a monk as Ganjin should be subjected to the jeopardy of a voyage fraught with peril?

Fushō eventually determined to set off alone. This meant that Yōei's death, as well as his own suffering during eight continuous years of wandering, had been in vain. At this juncture, however, he had no choice but to follow the way of his belief. The image of Gōgyō had begun to replace that of

Ganjin in his thoughts. There was no questioning the importance of transporting to Japan Gōgyō's vast accumulation of
Buddhist texts. Unfortunately a portion of it, never to touch
Japanese soil, had been left on an out-of-way island to the far
south of the empire. But a vast quantity still remained in
Gōgyō's possession, and Fushō believed he should dedicate
himself to the task of seeing it delivered in Japan.

These thoughts had crystalized gradually during the half-
year since Yōei's death, and they became decisive when Ganjin's eyesight began to fail rapidly during their sojourn in the
three monasteries in Shao-chou. Ganjin was then sixty-two.
Everyone except the young Ssu-ch'a had undergone marked
physical changes. The changes were registered not only in
their loss of strength but also in their faces. Because of his
advanced age Ganjin suffered most. The sooner he left the
party, Fushō thought, the sooner Ganjin could be taken
into the protective custody of the government.

Fushō informed Ganjin of his decision to separate himself
from the party and to proceed to the King Aśoka Monastery
in Mou-shan, where he would await passage to Japan. He
said he regretted not being able to sail together with Ganjin
for Japan, but he believed he should not be the cause of Ganjin's subjection to further wandering and deprivation. Ganjin
listened in silence, his eyes closed. He then opened his large
eyes and gazed intently at Fushō.

"I vowed to bring monastic discipline to Japan, and for
this I took to the sea several times. But I have not had the
good fortune to set foot on Japanese soil." Ganjin continued.
"Still, I must some day fulfill this vow. Right now, we are
traveling in the direction of Yang-chou. The years of wandering have taken their toll, and we are tired. Hsiang-yen's
health is impaired, and my own eyesight is failing. We must
return to Yang-chou to pause and rest before we can attempt
another voyage. That might be years hence. But your position is different, Fushō. If you stay with us, you will merely
be prolonging your stay in China, and to no useful purpose.
If you can find passage, you should return to Japan. We have
faced hardships together for a great many years, yet there
shall be no sailing for Japan together. I regret this, too."

Having said this, he beckoned Fushō to his side. Fushō

betook himself closer, and felt the venerable monk taking his hand into his own. His hand in Ganjin's grasp, Fushō wept.

On the day following, Fushō parted company with the monks who had been his companions through many years of adversity and suffering and set out alone for Mou-shan. He was escorted by Ssu-ch'a, who was loath to turn back. They walked together to a point some three miles beyond the city walls, and there they parted. It was summer, the month of June in 750. Fushō was past his mid-forties; Ssu-ch'a had just turned twenty-five.

11

Fushō arrived again at the King Aśoka Monastery in Mou-shan at the end of autumn. During those months of solitary travel, he had met with two remarkable experiences. The first occurred two months after he had left Shao-chou and was nearing Fu-chou. He had taken the road to Fu-chou, because it continued on to Wen-chou; from that point he would know the way to Mou-shan. He and Ganjin had taken that road some years ago, in 744.

He crossed the Great Yu-liang Range, then spent two months traveling through the alpine region before descending to the coastal plains. He continued on roads that were now level. Early one afternoon, clouds suddenly obscured the sun, and darkness settled about him. Though it was midsummer, a bleak wind rustled the leaves of the trees along the highway. Fushō was rooted to the ground within the darkened area.

"Fushō . . . " Unmistakably it was Ganjin's voice that he heard nearby. Startled, he looked about, but saw no one.

"Ganjin!" he shouted, transfixed. He wondered how Ganjin could have got there. The unaccountable strangeness was of short duration, and gradually the brightness of midday was restored. Ganjin was not, of course, anywhere to be seen. Could a mishap have befallen him? Fushō's thoughts were troubled; had he known that Ganjin was still in Shao-chou, he would have turned back at once. What had been portended was borne out, and Fushō was to learn later that a calamity had indeed befallen Ganjin during those moments.

After Fushō had left him, Ganjin's eyesight grew dimmer by the day, and he perceived objects only in hazy outlines. Urged by those about him, he risked treatment by a foreigner known for his skill at curing maladies of the eye. Not only was the treatment ineffective, but, worse, Ganjin was also blinded. It was when Ganjin lost his power of vision that Fushō found himself trapped in darkness and heard the venerable monk calling out to him.

The second remarkable occurrence came a month later. Fushō completed the trek along the coastal road from Fu-chou to Wen-chou, and at dusk had sought shelter in a ramshackle Zen temple in Wen-chou. Shortly before day-break he dreamed of Hsiang-yen. His friend was horri-bly gaunt. Hsiang-yen had never been robust, and when Fushō had last seen him, his health was failing and he was pitifully thin. But the man who came to him in his dream was worn to a shadow. Hsiang-yen approached wistful-ly, sat down beside him, and softly uttered, "Praise to Ami-tābha-buddha." And the dream was broken. Fushō sat up in bed, listening to the lingering echo of Hsiang-yen's voice. He was overcome with apprehension and felt a desperate concern for his friend. He was to learn subsequently that Hsiang-yen died about the time he had had that dream.

Death, which had snatched away Yōei, in the course of another few months was to take away Hsiang-yen. The monks had left the K'ai-yüan Monastery soon after Ganjin was afflicted with blindness. They visited the Ling-ch'iu and Kuang-kuo monasteries along the route to Chen-ch'ang District. From Chen-ch'ang they crossed over the precipi-tous Mei-ling Pass to the northern side and then sailed north on the Kan River to Ch'ien-chou; there they took lodging at the K'ai-yüan Monastery. Chung Shao-ch'ing, the former grand archivist of the empire, who had been living in re-tirement in that city, beseeched the monks to set up an ordination platform in his residence and administer the vows to him. They complied with his wishes, then boarded their vessel, sailed past Chi-chou, and approached the great Yangtze.

Toward dawn, Hsiang-yen suddenly sat up in his sickbed and asked whether Ganjin had awakened. Told by Ssu-ch'a that Ganjin had not yet risen, he said, "My life is about to expire. I wish to bid him farewell." Ssu-ch'a informed Ganjin, who rose promptly, lighted incense, and brought forth an arm rest to provide support for Hsiang-yen. Hsiang-yen was made to face the west and urged by Ganjin to invoke Amitābha. He did as he was told.

"Praise to Amitābha-buddha . . ." No more sounds came from his lips.

"Hsiang-yen! Yen!" Ganjin cried out. Hsiang-yen, still sitting erect, was dead. This was surely the moment that Hsiang-yen appeared in Fushō's dream.

Fushō arrived at the King Aśoka Monastery and rested a month. The years of continual wandering had been debilitating. Surrounded again by many friends, he felt as if he had returned home. Recollections of journeys across remote lands began to seem no more real than recollections of dreams.

His body well rested, Fushō set out for Lo-yang in order to meet with Gōgyō, who, according to Kaiyū, had taken up residence at the Great Fu-hsien Monastery. When he passed through Yang-chou, he heard nothing of Ganjin's having returned there.

Fushō was back in Lo-yang for the first time since 736, when he had left that capital with the entourage of Emperor Hsüan-tsung. He made his first visit in fourteen years to the Great Fu-hsien Monastery only to learn that his teacher Ting-p'in had died and that the monks he had known earlier no longer resided there. But he found Gōgyō at the monastery, as Kaiyū had said he would. Gōgyō lived in the quarters where the unfortunate aged Japanese monk named Keiun had once taken lodging. Fushō's arrival was announced by a resident monk, and Gōgyō appeared immediately. Indeed, his body had shrunk alarmingly. He seemed astonished when he recognized his visitor.

"Whatever happened?" he asked.

They went out into the garden, and as Fushō related in brief the story of their ill-fated sailing and the subsequent wandering, the expression on Gōgyō's face changed to one of anger, and his body trembled as he walked. Was he to understand, Gōgyō asked, that the texts he had placed in Fushō's care had been left at some nameless monastery in a region far to the south? He expressed this in his customary vague way of speaking, but his tone was bitterly critical.

"You may say it's nameless, Fushō replied, "but the Ta-yün Monastery is among the foremost Buddhist centers in Chen-chou. Your scrolls might have disintegrated on the ocean floor. Can't you now be content knowing they are somewhere in the land of China, contributing to the spread of Buddhist virtues?"

Fushō spoke gently, as if to an unreasoning child. He might have considered the censure offensive had it been uttered by someone other than Gōgyō. He had, after all, assured Gōgyō that the texts would be delivered to Japan but, instead, had deposited them on a remote island thousands of leagues to the south. Whatever the circumstances, he was accountable.

"Those texts were intended for Japan," Gōgyō countered. "As you've said, there may be some meaning in the fact that they're now at an out-of-the-way monastery that had previously no possessions other than Buddhist statues. Regardless, they're a part of what I've spent my life producing, and they were to be taken to Japan."

"Let me do this, then," Fushō said. "There is no telling how many years we may spend waiting for a ship to come from Japan. In the meantime, I'll make copies of the sutras that were left at the Ta-yün Monastery in Chen-chou. I'll make up the loss the best I can."

Fushō thought he could devote himself to the task until such time as they would find return passage to Japan. He would be doing this for Gōgyō, of course; but he also felt obligated to make this restitution for the purpose of advancing Buddhism in Japan. Gōgyō had retained a list of the titles of Buddhist texts that had been taken to the island of Hainan. Fushō made a copy of the list to take back with him to the King Aśoka Monastery in Mou-shan. As he returned he stopped briefly at Yang-chou, but again he heard nothing about Ganjin and his party of Buddhists.

At the King Aśoka Monastery, Fushō occupied a room facing a sparse grove of bamboo, which at one time may have been part of a garden. There he immersed himself in the work of transcribing sacred texts in order to discharge his obligation to Gōgyō. They were sutras that I-ching had translated into Chinese, and many of them were not to be found in Mou-shan. Fushō worked at transcribing whatever he could obtain.

In the spring of 751, Fushō learned of Ganjin's return to Yang-chou, but it was not until some years later that Ssu-ch'a could relate to him the following account of Ganjin's activities subsequent to his irreparable losses—of Yōei, his own eyesight, and Hsiang-yen, who had always been by him, like a shadow.

From Chi-chou, Ganjin's party continued down the Kan River, past Nan-ch'ang and Lake Poyang, in the direction of Chiang-chou, where the Kan flowed into the Yangtze. They broke their journey just short of the confluence in order to visit the Tung-lin Monastery at Mount Lu. The monastery was founded in the year 376 by the monk Hui-yüan of the Eastern Chin Dynasty. One day, as Hui-yüan was administering monastic vows on an altar he had installed, nectar rained down from the sky, and people thereafter referred to the altar as the Nectar Dais. The Nectar Dais still stood, and more recently, when the Teacher of the *Vinaya,* Chih-en, who was a disciple of Ganjin, was administering vows at the monastery, again the heavens sent down a rain of nectar. The dew that moistened the garments of those present was a sticky purple substance that tasted sweeter than honey. Everyone marveled at the fact that what they had witnessed was identical with the tradition associated with Hui-yüan. How true the Nectar Dais was to its name!

Ganjin spent three days at the monastery and took pleasure in listening to such tales about his former disciple. He then proceeded to the Lung-ch'üan Monastery in Hsin-yang, which had also been founded by Hui-yüan. Because there was no source of water when the monastery was first built, Hui-yüan uttered a supplication and then struck his ringed staff to the earth. A pair of blue dragons suddenly darted into the sky. The amazed onlookers then witnessed the sudden appearance of a spring that sent water gushing three feet into the air. Because of this legend, the monastery had been named the Lung-ch'üan, or "Dragon Spring," Monastery.

From Hsin-yang the party of monks proceeded overland

to the city of Chiang-chou (today, the port city of Kiukiang);
there they were greeted by the district governor and a throng
of Buddhists and Taoists, government officials, and members
of prominent families. Offerings of flowers were made, incense was burned, and music performed at the scene of the
welcome. They were entertained for three days, and on their
departure were escorted by the governor to Kiukiang.

The monks sailed east on the great Yangtze and in seven
days arrived at Chiang-ning (present-day Nanking) in Jun-
chou, where they visited the fabled sacred tower of the Wa-
kuan Monastery. The tower, erected by Emperor Wu of the
Liang Dynasty,* rose to a height of two hundred feet. It
had been standing for more than two centuries and was now
slightly tilted. According to legend, one morning following
a night-long tempest, people noticed footprints, apparently
of deities who must have stood at the four corners and held
the tower safely upright. At the four corners at the foot of
the tower, there now stood statues of the four deities as re-
minders of the event. The images measured three feet in
height and stood on bases embedded three inches below the
earth's surface. The sacred footprints that had given rise to the
legend were, at that time, still preserved.

Among the uncounted monasteries in Chiang-ning District, the party of monks visited those that had been built by
Emperor Wu of the Liang Dynasty: the Maitreya Temple
and the Chiang-ning, Ch'ang-ch'ing, and Yen-tze monasteries. Embellishments and sculpture at those sites were ex-
ecuted with consummate skill.

During their leisurely stay in Chiang-ning, the monks
received an unexpected visitor, Ling-yu, who at the time
held the incumbency of the Hsi-hsia Monastery on the foothills of nearby Mount She. When he came into Ganjin's
presence, Ling-yu fell to the ground and pressed his face
against Ganjin's feet.

"You left on a voyage eastward for the far-off country of
Japan, and I never expected to see you again," Ling-yu said,
his eyes filling with tears. "But here, today, I am once again
in your presence. I feel as if I am the proverbial blind turtle

*Reigned from 502 to 549.

that regained its sight and discovered the joy of seeing the
sun in the heavens once more. The spiritual light will again
shine brightly, and the gloom that once settled over the city
streets will surely be dispelled.''

Ganjin's wrath toward Ling-yu, the well-intentioned informant, had since been dispelled, and he consented to be
escorted to Ling-yu's monastery.

The Hsi-hsia-ssu was founded by Ming Seng-chao, who
converted his residence into a monastery in 489, the seventh
year of the Yung-ming Era of the Ch'i Dynasty. It was renowned because both Hui-pu and Hui-feng, celebrated
monks of the Three Treatises Sect, had resided there. More
recently, three of Ganjin's disciples, Hsüan-kuang, Hsi-yu,
and T'an-pi, had been in residence there from time to time.
Thus there were ties that bound Ganjin to this monastery.

The monks left Mount She three days later and took the
road that would lead them, at long last, back to Yang-chou.
They crossed the Yangtze and sailed past Kua-chou to the
New Canal.

At the far end of the plain before them they saw the city
walls of their cherished Yang-chou. Rather than proceed
directly into the city, they went to the Chi-ch'i Monastery.
This was where they had gathered to plan their very first
voyage, and every tree, every blade of grass on the grounds
had emotional meaning for them.

When the clergy and citizens of the great metropolis on the
Yangtze learned about Ganjin's return, they streamed from
the city to greet him. The road was thronged and the canal
congested with vessels carrying well-wishers to the monastery.

The monks were soon back inside the city, and Ganjin
again took up residence in the Lung-hsing Monastery. With
a look of determination ever present in his uplifted face, he
lectured on the *Vinaya* and administered monastic vows
just as he had done years earlier, quite as if he no longer remembered his recent trials. The only discernible difference
was in his eyes, hollow in their sockets and no longer seeing.

12

From spring through the summer of 751 at the King

Aśoka Monastery, Fushō occupied himself daily with the task of transcribing Buddhist texts. He had known since he began the work that Ganjin was already in Yang-chou, but he did not go there. He was concerned lest his presence in Yang-chou disturb Ganjin's peace. Besides, he was reluctant to spend precious time traveling. Not until he had actually begun transcribing did he realize how much effort and time he would have to devote to this incredibly difficult task. What he could accomplish in a day, though he worked from dawn to dusk, seemed pitifully meager.

One day Fushō was told that Ganjin was lecturing and administering monastic vows not only at the Lung-hsing-ssu, but also at the Ch'ung-fu, Ta-ming, and Yen-kuang monasteries. He had many occasions that day to lay down his writing brush, gaze out of his dim room at the brightness without, and think of him. He knew that Ganjin had lost his eyesight, but, try as he would, he could not visualize Ganjin existing in darkness.

A year passed, and Fushō was still awaiting a vessel bound for Japan. He was no longer certain whether he really looked forward to finding passage to Japan. He was aware that in one respect he had begun to resemble Gōgyō. He had transcribed more than thirty scrolls during the previous year, only half of his obligation. "May no ship come until I've finished the rest," he thought anxiously. As he realized the contradiction in his own thinking, he came also to realize that the confused look Gōgyō habitually wore was not, as they had all thought, due to any irresolution.

Fushō left for Lo-yang at the beginning of the new year. He needed to ask Gōgyō where to find translations by I-ching that he could not obtain at the King Aśoka Monastery. Before, Fushō had never failed to see Gōgyō at his desk, busily transcribing texts, but when Fushō arrived this time at the Great Fu-hsien Monastery he found the aging monk lying sick in bed.

Fushō asked Gōgyō where he might acquire the *Sutra of Invocations Praising the Virtues of the Tathāgata* and eleven other sacred texts, twenty-one scrolls in all, translated by I-ching in the year 711 at the Great Fu-hsien-ssu. Because all monasteries Gōgyō named were in Ch'ang-an, Fushō asked whether he might not obtain them in either Lo-yang or Yang-chou, for, if at all possible, he would like to be spared the added travel to Ch'ang-an.

"I wouldn't know," Gōgyō replied. "Do you realize how difficult it is to acquire sutras? Why, I've traveled between the eastern and western capitals time and again to obtain just one sutra."

His remark suggested quite clearly his disapproval of what he considered Fushō's laggardness. Gōgyō had displayed ill-humor during their previous meeting, and he had grown more sullen in the year since. There were no longer traces of the child-like innocence that had once characterized him. Only crankiness, brought on by old age, was etched into the deeply wrinkled face. Gōgyō had spent most of his life in an alien land, absorbed only in transcribing sacred texts, and his appearance was indeed that of a man who had trod this chosen path to its ultimate.

Fushō was aware of Gōgyō's persistent bitterness over his having abandoned the two crates of scrolls on Hainan Island. But he understood why Gōgyō continued to nourish his anger with self-pity, for the aged monk had poured his lifeblood and soul into those scrolls.

Fushō left Lo-yang and was soon in Ch'ang-an. A full decade had flown by since the time he set out from Ch'ang-an in 742 with Japan as his destination. Everything he saw in the capital evoked fond recollections. He went to the Ch'ung-fu Monastery, where he had once been assigned quarters as a student-monk from a foreign land. As he walked through the towered gate, he recalled the excitement of the days when he first read such writings as Fa Li's *Annotation of the Vinaya Canon* and Ting-p'in's commentary to the *Annotation*. There were several monks at the monastery whom he had known before, and they seemed surprised to learn that he had not yet left China.

When Fushō learned that the monastery possessed copies of the writings he needed, he sought to borrow them. His request was denied, for he was no longer registered as a student-monk from abroad; nor could he claim the status of a naturalized monk, a courtesy accorded only to duly registered foreign monks after eight years of residence in China.

He conceived the stratagem of utilizing Abé Nakamaro to gain access to the sacred texts. Nakamaro was then Supervisor of the Palace Gate Guards, a high post that carried with it the concurrent directorships of the bureaus of Armory, Weapons and Machines, and Palace Guards; he held the administrative reins of both military and cultural affairs in the government. He mingled with such luminaries as Li Po and Wang Wei* and was himself a celebrated literary figure. During the decade Fushō had spent wandering about China, Nakamaro's name had acquired distinction both at court and in the world of letters. Fushō had once had an occasion to meet with him in Lo-yang at the office of the Central Ministry on the imperial palace grounds, but now it was no simple matter to arrange a meeting. Fushō's message passed through the hands of several officials before it reached Nakamaro, and the reply was sent down to him through the same bureaucratic route. In four days he could see Nakamaro.

The two met in an office that was part of a complex of government offices situated at the top of a rise. Nakamaro was expressionless, as he had been at their meeting more than a decade earlier. He looked slightly away from Fushō, as though he wished only to hear his words; presently, he nodded, and then again, as if he fully understood what Fushō was trying to convey. Offering the excuse of business elsewhere, he stood up abruptly and led the way out of the room.

Fushō was dismayed by the seemingly cold and capricious attitude of the old man, and was convinced that the conversation had served no useful purpose. The next day, however, an official in Nakamaro's service brought him a message indicating that his requests had been fulfilled. Indeed, as Fushō soon learned, every arrangement had been made in his behalf.

Until summer, in the seclusion of a room in the dormitory of the Ch'ung-fu Monastery, Fushō devoted himself to

*Two of the most illustrious among the brilliant array of T'ang poets of the eighth century.

transcribing the *Sutra of Invocations Praising the Virtues of the Tathāgata* and several other sacred texts. During that period he made many inquiries regarding Genrō's whereabouts, but could learn nothing.

In July a monk from Lo-yang brought these tidings: four ships from Japan had touched land at Ming-chou and deposited members of an ambassadorial mission safely on T'ang soil. Fushō was startled by the news. This mission, the tenth to the court of T'ang, had been dispatched after an interval of nineteen years.

Within a month's time the news of the arrival of the Japanese mission was being circulated throughout the city. Fushō was now reluctant to divert even a moment to a task other than that of transcribing sutras. The embassy was already in China, and the ships that had brought the Japanese would be leaving soon, surely during the coming year. The feeling of urgency compelled Fushō to stay at his desk and work continually.

13

In 750 the Japanese imperial court in the city of Nara decided to dispatch the tenth ambassadorial mission to the T'ang court. Seventeen years had passed since Tajihi Hironari had led the previous mission to China. On the twenty-fourth of September, Fujiwara Kiyokawa was designated ambassador, and Ōtomo Komaro vice-ambassador; appointees to the posts of praetor and scribe were also designated. In November, Kibi Makibi, who had returned to Japan on a ship of the previous mission, was appointed to share the post of vice-ambassador with Ōtomo Komaro.

It was not until two years later, however, that Fujiwara Kiyokawa was summoned to the Inner Palace to receive the ambassadorial sword; the event took place on the ninth day of the intercalary month of March in 752. Empress Kōmyō on that occasion addressed this poem to the ambassador-elect:

On a great ship
With many oars to guide it true,
This child mine

I send to the land of China.
Succor him, o *kami!*

Kiyokawa replied in kind:

O plum blossoms
Of the revered shrine, so sacred
To Kasuga Plain,
Stay in full flower, awaiting
The day of my return.

The commander of the gate guardians, Ōtomo Kojihi, honored the vice-ambassador Ōtomo Komaro, his kin, with a splendid banquet at his residence.

To this stalwart,
Bound for the land of China
With sure promise
Of fulfillment and return,
I offer this wine.

This poem, included in *A Collection of a Myriad Leaves*, was addressed to the guest of honor by Tajihi Takanushi.

More than five hundred men set sail in four ships from the bay of Naniwa in late spring. They touched land in the vicinity of Ning-po in July, and arrived in Ch'ang-an in late autumn. No sooner did Fushō hear about their arrival than he hastened to the Hung-lu-ssu (the quarters for official guests) in order to greet the men who had brought with them the scent of his native land. He met with Kiyokawa, Komaro, and Makibi.

Ambassador Kiyokawa, a man whose refined features and restrained dignity bespoke a noble lineage, asked Fushō about his experiences during his lengthy stay in the T'ang empire. Fushō recounted the hardships he had shared with Ganjin during their years of wandering about China, but he found the Japanese ambassador, a man about his own age, not at all impressed. Neither was the vice-ambassador Kibi Makibi moved by his account. Fushō and Makibi had met twenty years before at the Ssu-fang House in Lo-yang. Makibi, having completed his studies, was then preparing to return to Japan. He had no recollection, however, of their previous meeting. Fushō recalled having been impressed by Makibi's serenity and poise—qualities that made him appear Chinese —but he could no longer find those traits in him. Makibi had become a somewhat arrogant, self-satisfied, humorless old man.

In Japan, Makibi had enjoyed the unusual success of rising to the post of commander of officers of the right guards. He was now approaching sixty. He asked Fushō a few questions concerning the monks from Japan, their methods of study, and the subject matters that interested them. Fushō was certain his answer would disappoint the eminent statesman; nonetheless, he related what he knew. Yōei had died during their wandering; Kaiyū, when he had last seen him in Canton, had talked of travel to India but had not been heard from since then; Genrō had relegated himself to obscurity. What a difference compared with Makibi, who had distinguished himself in China as an exceptionally brilliant student from abroad! Fushō noticed a hint of derision reflected in his eyes.

Makibi must have known of Ganjin's preëminence. Yet he remained expressionless as Fushō described the tribulations that Ganjin had been subjected to over the course of many years.

"So long as a voyage is feasible and preparations are adequate," Makibi said, "a ship should cross the sea without incident. In order to set a ship on a course to Japan, you must take advantage of all the elements—the moon, stars, wind, and sea. If you allow the elements to work against you, never can you steer a ship toward Japanese waters."

He seemed irritated that their sailing should have gone awry. What he said was in character, for when he was a student in China Makibi had studied the classics and histories, as well as the secrets of divination, calendric science, and mathematics—and had mastered them all.

Only Ōtomo Komaro paid heed to Fushō. "If Ganjin, or whatever his name is, is so intent on getting to Japan, perhaps we should take him back with us," he said, addressing his remarks to no particular person. Komaro alone appeared to have been moved by Fushō's story, though he apparently was neither informed of Ganjin's eminence nor aware of the significance of seeing orthodox monasticism introduced to Japan.

After leaving the Hung-lu-ssu, Fushō walked about the streets of Ch'ang-an, a city he had not visited in many years. He overheard a merchant remarking that Premier Li Lin-fu had died, and the news touched him deeply. Fushō had not seen the prime minister since that day in an era long past, it seemed, when he had enlisted his aid in planning the first of their sailings.

During the next several months, until the spring of 753, Fushō worked continually in his room at the Ch'ung-fu Monastery. During that time, he was sought out by young monks only recently arrived on the ships of the embassy mission. He thought back to the time when he had first come to the T'ang empire and had gone immediately to see Keiun and Gōgyō, and he wondered whether he appeared as listless and crestfallen in the eyes of these newcomers as Keiun and Gōgyō had once appeared in his.

Fushō was able to learn much from the young Japanese monks. When the Japanese ambassador's party was granted an audience at the palace, Emperor Hsüan-tsung expressed his pleasure at receiving emissaries from a nation that observed proprieties in matters of ritual and sovereignty. Abé Nakamaro, assigned by the Emperor as guide for the ambassador's party, escorted them to the Hall of the Three Teachings, where the scriptures of Confucianism, Taoism, and Buddhism were stored, and to the principal Buddhist monasteries among the countless many that occupied the one hundred and ten city blocks of the capital. At the formal New Year reception at the imperial palace, Kiyokawa, Komaro, and Makibi disputed the order of seating with the emissaries from the Korean kingdom of Silla; because of Komaro's insistence, the Japanese were able to occupy the position of honor among all foreign emissaries.

The news that Li Lin-fu had posthumously been divested of his rank and honors stirred Fushō much more deeply than reports of the posturing and ostentation of the Japanese in

Ch'ang-an. The action against Li Lin-fu came in consequence of the discovery of a rebellious intent he was said to have harbored against Hsüan-tsung; but the affair was shrouded in an unhealthy atmosphere of political intrigue. Every member of Li's clan was affected in some way in the aftermath. Fushō recalled the remark Yōei had made twenty years earlier— that he detected a vague aura of decay and doom about the government and culture of the great T'ang civilization. Fushō himself could now detect it.

As early as March there was talk of the Japanese mission's departure. The ambassador's party planned to leave Ch'ang-an for the port of embarkation at the onset of autumn. There were rumors that Abé Nakamaro would at last terminate his stay in China in order to return with the ambassador's party to his homeland.

These stories prompted Fushō to consider leaving Ch'ang-an at once. He would have to see Gōgyō at the Great Fu-hsien-ssu in Lo-yang to make certain he would be ready for the sailing, and then hasten back to the King Aśoka Monastery to make his own preparations for departure. Fortunately his task of transcribing Buddhist texts was almost completed.

Two days before leaving Ch'ang-an, Fushō called on Ōtomo Komaro and explained to him the significance of having Ganjin taken to Japan. His presence there would mean that Japan, for the first time, would be introduced to orthodox ordination rituals; as a result, Buddhism, transmitted to Japan two centuries earlier, would at long last assume its total form. Komaro listened attentively and then told Fushō to give him the names of other monks who should be invited to Japan.

Fushō named five others: Ssu-ch'a, who was then said to be in residence at the K'ai-yüan-ssu in T'ai-chou; Fa-chin of Po-t'a-ssu in Yang-chou; T'an-ching of Ch'ao-kung-ssu in Ch'üan-chou; I-ching* of Hsin-yün-ssu in Yang-chou; and Fa-ts'ai of Ling-shaō-ssu in Ch'ü-chou. They were monks whose dedication to the teachings of the *Vinaya* had earned them Fushō's admiration. Ssu-ch'a, Fa-ts'ai, and T'an-ching

---

*Not to be confused with I-ching, the famous translator of Indian Buddhist texts.

were the three who had stayed beside Ganjin during the many arduous years of wandering that began with their first attempt in 742 to cross the seas to Japan. Komaro intended to petition Emperor Hsüan-tsung directly to obtain permission to take the Chinese monks to Japan. Fushō left Ch'ang-an before Komaro could memorialize the Emperor. He thought it best to delegate the responsibility of making these arrangements to the ambassador's party. Ganjin would make his own decision as to whether he would sail with the Japanese mission.

Fushō set out from Ch'ang-an at the end of April. He climbed the hill that rose beyond the north wall of the city and surveyed the whole of the capital—the nine avenues and twelve boulevards, which he would never see again—all lush with new greenery. He then descended the hill and left Ch'ang-an behind him.

In Lo-yang, Fushō went immediately to the Great Fu-hsien Monastery, informed Gōgyō of what he had accomplished in two years' time, and urged him to begin preparing at once for the sailing, which very likely would be during the year. Having learned that the once-lost Buddhist texts would be restored to him, Gōgyō became surprisingly docile. His anger at Fushō had been dispelled, and he seemed willing to have Fushō make the decisions that would govern his few remaining years and determine the fate of his vast collection of Buddhist writings.

Fushō instructed Gōgyō to bring all his transcribed texts, scattered about in various caches, to the Ch'an-chih Monastery in Yang-chou. He then left Lo-yang and returned directly to the King Aśoka Monastery in Mou-shan, to await the day of his return to Japan. He was to be notified of the sailing as soon as the date was set.

During Fushō's long sojourn in China, the days spent at the King Aśoka Monastery were the times of his greatest contentment. Assured now of returning to Japan, he could indulge himself in leisure and unconcern as he awaited the forthcoming sailing. Fushō was nearing the age of fifty and preferred the calm and quiet of Mou-shan to Ch'ang-an, Lo-yang, or Yang-chou. He was fond of the deteriorating temple that boasted an illustrious past. He found pleasure in seeing the sun's lambent rays on the desolate garden and in hearing the breeze rustle the bamboo groves.

One day, Fushō saw a visitor entering the garden. He did not recognize the man at once, but in a few moments he asked softly, "Is that you, Genrō?" Attired in Chinese garb, Genrō was, to all appearances, a Chinese.

"How I've wanted to see you!" His tone conveyed fully the pain of yearning. A confusion of emotions registered in his face, and he seemed about to break into sobs.

"I came to ask a favor of you," Genrō said, once they had exchanged appropriate greetings. He was no longer the handsome man he had been in youth. His attire was not that of a cleric, and his hair was groomed in secular fashion. Although he did not look shabby, the shadowy traits of a forsaken, lonely man were easily discernible.

When Fushō invited him into his room, Genrō asked if he might have his companions join him. He went out to the garden, and some moments later returned together with a middle-aged woman, plain but gentle in disposition, and two girls, both about ten years of age. They were his wife and children. The woman offered a few words of greeting but did not come into the room; she said that her children wished to play outside, and went back to the garden with them.

Genrō said he had come to inquire whether there might be a way for him to return to Japan together with his wife and two children. "Although I came to China as a student-monk, I've accomplished nothing in twenty years' time," he said rather dejectedly. "I've forgotten whatever I may have learned during my first few years here. All I can call my own are a wife and children whose complexion and features are quite unlike mine. With money I would be able to contribute to the store of commodities to be taken back to Japan by the mission, but I have no money. Yet I do want to return to Japan. I want my wife and daughters to see the country where I was born and grew up."

Genrō seemed sadly troubled, and Fushō could offer no consoling words. Had Genrō remained unmarried, even though giving himself wholly to dissipation during his stay as a student-monk, he might have been able to present some kind of alibi upon returning to Japan. Accompanied by a wife and children, however, his circumstances would be difficult. Even if he managed the return, accompanied by his family, there would be resentment and he would surely be reproached.

"I don't know whether you can obtain permission," Fushō said, "but I will speak to those who are in charge."

He would have to wait until the ambassador's party arrived at the port of embarkation before he could present such a request. He instructed Genrō to stay in Yang-chou with his family, to anticipate a message that would be sent to the Ch'an-chih Monastery, and to be prepared to board ship at any given moment.

Genrō had traveled a considerable distance to Mou-shan in order to ask this favor of Fushō, but he rose to leave as soon as they had finished discussing the matter. Not having seen Genrō for many years, Fushō wished that they might dine together and enjoy a leisurely conversation; but Genrō appeared ill at ease. He told Fushō that he and his family had already taken a room at an inn.

"I must be off today," he said, and departed in haste.

Fushō remained seated on the veranda and let his thoughts wander for a long while. If Genrō were to be judged as a student-monk, he could, of course, be censured for having chosen the way of errantry. If he were to be judged simply as a man, however, he seemed to be without character defects of any consequence. Fushō and Yōei had dedicated their stay in China to the task of bringing Ganjin to Japan; had they not been thus preoccupied, they, too, might have fallen victim to the same pitfall. A difference of a hair's breadth had allowed of quite different fates.

Genrō had taken up with a foreign woman, but he honored the relationship; he would not have considered abandoning his wife and children in order to return to his homeland. He wished to take them back to the land and people he so fondly remembered. For Genrō's sake as well, Fushō thought, he must leave Mou-shan as soon as he was notified of the date of the sailing.

cf. modern Taiwanese attitudes towards Japanese

14

When the date of their departure from Ch'ang-an had been

set, members of the Japanese mission formally petitioned Emperor Hsüan-tsung regarding Ganjin and the five other Buddhists. The Emperor did not object to Ganjin's leaving China, but he insisted upon Taoists being taken to Japan along with the Buddhists. This presented a dilemma that threatened delay. Hsüan-tsung revered Lao-tzu and was partial to Taoist teachings, but the non-Buddhist philosophy had not yet been introduced into Japan. The Japanese had to withdraw their request. Moreover, lest their actions incur Imperial displeasure, they assigned Shun Tōgen and three others to remain in China to study the Way of the Taoists. The means of taking Ganjin to Japan would have to be sought elsewhere.

Ambassador Kiyokawa and his party departed from Ch'ang-an at the end of summer. When they broke their travel at Yang-chou, four of them—Kiyokawa, Komaro, Makibi, and Abé Nakamaro, who had been granted permission to return to Japan—called on Ganjin at the Yen-kuang Monastery and informed him of recent happenings.

Komaro said to Ganjin: "We would like you to devise some suitable means." He was implying that Ganjin's leaving China would not be overtly sanctioned; nevertheless, he would be welcome aboard any of the four great ships, all fitted and ready for sailing. Ganjin nodded in satisfaction and told them that his five previous attempts to sail to Japan had ended in failure, but that he now entertained the hope that these ships from Japan would enable him to fulfill his wish.

The fact that four members of the Japanese mission had visited Ganjin attracted notice, and rumor was soon widespread in the city of Yang-chou that Ganjin was again planning to sail to Japan. As a result, the government took steps to increase the surveillance over the Lung-hsing Monastery, where Ganjin had taken up residence in order to make preparations for the voyage.

On the second of October, Fushō arrived in Yang-chou from the King Aśoka Monastery in Mou-shan. He went directly to the Ch'an-chih Monastery, where he and Gōgyō had agreed to meet. He saw the dozen or more boxes into which Gōgyō had packed his scrolls, ready for transport at any time. There was yet no message from Genrō. On the following day, Fushō sought out Ōtomo Komaro in order to discuss Genrō's predicament. Although he had anticipated difficulties, passage to Japan for Genrō was arranged with surprising ease.

From Komaro, Fushō learned that Ganjin was determined to sail for Japan and that he would slip away from the Lung-hsing Monastery at the first opportunity, proceed to the port of Huang-ssu-p'u, and board one of the ships of the Japanese mission. Despite his eagerness to see Ganjin and to serve him, Fushō resisted the temptation to go to the Lung-hsing Monastery, for the cloister appeared to be under close surveillance, and his presence there could very well disrupt carefully laid plans.

The date for boarding drew near, but still there was no word from Genrō. Passage had been arranged for the family of four, and they needed only to be present; but they did not appear. Perhaps Genrō had despaired of obtaining permission to return to Japan. Perhaps he was beset by other doubts and had become hesitant at the last moment. Fushō was beside himself with anxiety. The four ships of the embassy to T'ang were scheduled to sail away from Huang-ssu-p'u in mid-November; the voyagers must be at the port by the end of October.

The Japanese mission departed Yang-chou for Huang-ssu-p'u in three separate groups, the first leaving on the thirteenth of October and the others following at two-day intervals. Gōgyō, with his ponderous load of religious texts, was aboard the vessel that carried the second group. Fushō intended to wait for Genrō until the last moment and sail from Yang-chou with the third group. As he was about to board ship, however, he was informed by Komaro that Ganjin and his party of monks were planning to leave on the night of the nineteenth. He decided to sail with Ganjin's party, for then he could remain two more days in Yang-chou.

According to Komaro, a disciple of Ganjin by the name of Jen-kan of Wu-chou (present-day Chin-hua in Chekiang

Province) had learned of the planned voyage and agreed to bring a vessel to the head of the canal under cover of night in order to transport Ganjin's party to Huang-ssu-p'u.

Fushō remained at the Ch'an-chih Monastery until nightfall on the nineteenth, but still he received no word from Genrō. There was nothing more he could do. He left the city of Yang-chou alone and took the road leading to the waterfront. He easily found Jen-ken's vessel, but Ganjin and his party had not yet arrived. Fushō passed two restless hours aboard the vessel; then he heard footsteps approaching out of the darkness. He stepped off the boat onto the embankment. It was not Ganjin's party but a group of twenty-four Buddhist acolytes. They had come to receive blessings from Ganjin, whom they could never hope to see again, for he would soon be sailing eastward across the broad expanse.

Another hour, and this time it was Ganjin and his party of monks approaching. Fushō stood on the embankment and called his own name. "Fushō!" The voice of the eminent monk also called out from the darkness. Fushō walked to the source of that voice and took the hand of his teacher. As he had in the summer of 750, when the two bade each other farewell at the K'ai-yüan Monastery in Shao-chou, Fushō felt the touch of Ganjin's big-boned, wrinkled hands on his face, then on his shoulders and chest. He was overcome by a surge of emotion and was unable to speak.

Ganjin administered the Supreme Clerical Vow to the twenty-four acolytes, and then took his party aboard the ship. They cast off immediately to begin a leisurely descent of the great river.

Myriad thoughts crowded Fushō's mind. This marked his third sailing down the Yangtze together with Ganjin, with Japan as their destination. The first time they set sail, in December of 743, was on a moonlit night; but their second sailing, in June of 747, had been undertaken on a night as dark as this. Their first sailing had taken place ten years before, and six years had passed since their second departure.

Fushō learned, once aboard the vessel, that Ganjin was accompanied by the five monks whose names he had given to Komaro—Ssu-ch'a, Fa-chin, T'an-ching, I-ching, and Fa-ts'ai. The party included nine other monks, Fa-ch'eng of the K'ai-yüan Monastery of Tou-chou being one among them, and ten lay persons, Chinese as well as men from Siberia, Champa, and the Malayan region. They carried very little with them. The many possessions that would accompany Ganjin to Japan had already been transported in several consignments to the port of embarkation.

Fushō was anxious to see Ganjin's face—and Ssu-ch'a's and Fa-ts'ai's and T'an-ching's—but until dawn he had to content himself with hearing their voices. He awoke at daybreak; at last, he could look upon the face of his blind teacher. Ganjin sat with his back against the rail, his head tilted slightly upward. Was he asleep? His face should have borne traces of the passage of three years' time, but, in fact, it had acquired a youthful cast. Although he was totally blind, there were no signs of brooding or melancholy in his countenance. The fiery element in his personality, which Fushō had associated with the character of the ancient warrior, was gone, and the revered monk, then sixty-five, appeared serene and radiant.

Ganjin turned abruptly toward Fushō, some six yards away. Seen full, his face expressed calm, yet retained the strength of will that had always characterized it.

"Did you sleep well, Fushō?" he asked.

"I just opened my eyes, but how could you have known?" Fushō answered, surprised.

Ganjin laughed. "I am blind, so how could I have known? I've called to you several times already." Fushō did not laugh. He turned his face, wet with tears, toward the chilling wind that swept the river at dawn.

"Fushō, are you weeping?" Ganjin asked, although not a sound had escaped Fushō's lips.

"No," he replied steadily. "I am not."

The other monks were soon awake. Ssu-ch'a retained no trace whatever of his former youthful bearing, but had acquired the dignity and poise that befitted a monk who ranked high among the senior disciples of Ganjin. Both Fa-ts'ai and T'an-ching appeared hardier now—in contrast to the gauntness of that period of wandering in south China. Now that he was reunited with the Chinese monks, Fushō was sad, for missing among them were Yōei and Hsiang-yen, with whom he had shared hardships during the many years of wandering.

Once they were at Huang-ssu-p'u, each busied himself with the task of loading the second and third ships with commodities destined for Japan. Among the important Buddhist statues taken aboard were the Tathāgata-Amita, the Thousand-armed Avalokita carved of white sandalwood, an embroidered image of the Thousand-armed Avalokita, the World-Savior Avalokita, the teacher of medicine Bhaiṣaj-yaguru, Amitābha, and the bodhisattva Maitreya. The volume of religious texts was staggering.* Fushō was familiar with many of them; he had, after all, begrudged himself even sleep in order to study them during the first of the two decades he had spent in the T'ang empire. The *Record of Western Regions* by the monk Hsüan-tsang, the last item of the catalogue shown him by Ssu-ch'a, was a book Kaiyū had talked about when they had last met in Canton.

The catalogue of goods listed, in addition, an infinite variety of treasures, such as "three thousand grains of Buddha's mortal remains," ceremonial equipment, and religious paintings. An entry that arrested Fushō's attention was "one set of gold-and-copper stupas, modeled on the King Aśoka Stupa."

On the twenty-third of October, it was announced that the two dozen men in Ganjin's company would be boarding separate vessels. Ganjin and the fourteen monks traveling with him would sail aboard the lead ship along with Ambassador Kiyokawa; the ten others in his party would accompany Makibi on the third ship. Gōgyō and Fushō would travel with Komaro on the second ship.

Fushō quite unexpectedly received a letter from Genrō that day. It was delivered to him by a boatman who had come to Huang-ssu-p'u from Yang-chou. Genrō asked forgiveness for having failed to meet him at the Ch'an-chih Monastery as he had promised. He confessed that, though he could scarcely endure his yearning for Japan, it was presumptuous of him to hope of ever returning; he would accept his deserved end and live out his life in China. The message was brief. Ac-

*Omitted here is an enumeration of two dozen titles of Buddhist texts and commentaries.

cording to the boatman, Genrō was staying in a shop in the market area in the southeastern section of Yang-chou.

Fushō read the letter over and over. Evidently Genrō had changed his mind because he was ashamed of his predicament; Fushō became convinced of this. He must make every effort to have Genrō return with them to Japan. So long as the scheduled mid-November sailing date remained unchanged, he should have sufficient time to return to Yang-chou to fetch Genrō and his family.

He discussed the plan immediately with Komaro. That Genrō had forsaken the clergy or had failed to acquire learning was of little concern to Komaro, who was inclined to think that Genrō's having a Chinese wife made him potentially more valuable as a returnee than men who had stuffed their minds with random bits of information. He seemed incapable of understanding Genrō's hesitancy.

"He must be a fool," Komaro said. "There's nothing to be done if he doesn't want to go back to Japan. But if he does, you ought to go to Yang-chou and use force, if necessary, to bring him here."

Fushō left at once. Owing to Genrō's plight he was again able to set foot in Yang-chou. It was near the end of October, and the leaves of elm and pagoda trees were lightly tinged with yellow. Fushō went to the shop in the market area where Genrō was said to be staying, only to learn that Genrō and his family had departed two days before for Ch'ang-an. He was bitterly disappointed. With time running short, he had taken special pains to retrace his way from the port, but the effort had been wholly wasted.

Although he intended to return immediately to Huang-ssu-p'u, the travel-weary monk suddenly developed a fever and had to spend five days in sickbed at an inn in Yang-chou. Anxiety preyed on his mind even as he lay ill. The moment the fever abated, Fushō, driving his still languid body relentlessly, began the arduous trek back to the port. He arrived at Huang-ssu-p'u on the thirteenth of November.

Fushō found all the members of Ganjin's party gathered aboard the second ship, which was under Komaro's command, though originally they had been assigned to the lead and third vessels. There had been an unexpected turn of events during his absence. Ganjin's party had gone aboard the day Fushō left for Yang-chou, but very soon thereafter, they had been ordered to disembark. Some members of the mission, it developed, were fearful of Kuang-ling County officials being informed of the projected voyage of the Buddhists. If a search were made and Ganjin apprehended aboard a ship of the Japanese mission, the consequences would be grave. Should they succeed in putting out to sea with the monks aboard, the secret would be disclosed if the ships ever failed of their course and touched again on Chinese soil. Under the circumstances, it seemed sensible to remove the monks from the ships. Other opinions were presented, but Ambassador Kiyokawa accepted the argument favoring precaution and ordered Ganjin and his party off the ships.

Bewildered by the unexpected turn of events that apparently thwarted their plan to sail for Japan, Ganjin and his men lingered in Huang-ssu-p'u. It was Komaro who came to their rescue. Taking matters entirely into his own hands, on the night of the tenth of November, three days before Fushō returned, he took aboard his ship all twenty-four men. Because of the resultant overcrowding of the second ship, Fushō and Gōgyō were reassigned to the third ship.

There had been another controversy during Fushō's absence. Gōgyō insisted on his Buddhist texts being carried aboard the ship on which he was to sail, and this required the transfer of crates containing the innumerable scrolls. The task would be a nuisance to members of the crew, harrassed as they were by the work of fitting the ships for imminent voyage. Many attempted to reason with Gōgyō, but he would not be dissuaded. He ultimately obtained his wish to the great unhappiness of the crew.

Fushō went aboard the third ship and found Gōgyō alone near the stern, surrounded by several dozen boxes packed tightly with his transcriptions. The monk appeared to have narrowly managed to eke out a space for himself amid the stacks.

On the night of the fourteenth, Fushō visited Ganjin and Ssu-ch'a aboard the second vessel. They would be sailing across the great expanse on separate ships, and they could not know whether the same end had been foreordained for all.

The ships weighed anchor together and set sail under bright moonlight on the night of the fifteenth. On that night Abé Nakamaro, on board the lead vessel, leaving China after a stay of thirty-six years, composed his celebrated poem:

> Scanning the celestial expanse,
> I see the moon . . .
> Is it the same moon
> That rises over Mikasa Mountain
> In my beloved Kasuga?

Homeward bound, the ships of the Japanese mission to the T'ang empire left the shore of Huang-ssu-p'u in prescribed order—the lead vessel followed by the second, third, and fourth ships. They had been cruising down the Yangtze close to an hour when a pheasant was seen winging before the helm of the lead vessel. Like a tiny black object hurtled into the night sky, the bird described a line of flight that cut across the path of the ship at mast-height and streaked across the glistening expanse of the moonlit Yangtze. Only a few men aboard the lead vessel saw the pheasant. The shipmaster regarded this strange phenomenon as an ill omen. A signal was flashed to the third ship, then sailing directly behind the lead vessel, and eventually all four vessels cast anchor and remained in midstream through the night.

On the morning of the sixteenth, the four ships were again under way. Fortunately the wind was still, and the surface of the river was calm. Yet hardly two hours had passed before the ships departed the order of sail, and the second ship drifted into the lead. In that wise the four vessels continued down the murky flow toward the estuary.

15

Around midnight of the twentieth of November, the sixth day after setting sail from Huang-ssu-p'u, the third ship, carrying Vice-Ambassador Makibi and Fushō and Gōgyō, arrived safely at the island of Okinawa. During the first three days of sailing, this group of voyagers had kept the lead and second vessels in sight, though they were quite some distance before them, and the fourth ship as well, which sailed far behind in their wake. When the fourth day dawned, however, the other ships had disappeared from view, and they had sailed on alone to Okinawa.

At dusk on the day following their arrival, the lead ship of Ambassador Kiyokawa came into the same port; closely following her was the second ship, with Vice-Ambassador Komaro at the helm. All voyagers disembarked the next day and congratulated one another on their good fortune. But there was much concern among them over the fate of the fourth ship.

The sea became turbulent the day after. Waves mounted the tall cliffs and burst into white foam. Great flocks of exotic birds sailed above the stormy sea in migratory flight. The departure of all three vessels from Okinawa was postponed until such time as total calm should prevail.

The voyagers left their ships frequently to explore the island. Over the tempestuous sea the sky was a canopy of brilliant azure; the whitish soil and the betel palms that overspread much of the island were bathed in sunlight that seemed unseasonably bright. Fushō and Ssu-ch'a wandered about the island together, searching out areas quite distant from the port. Just as he had done years earlier, Ssu-ch'a made detailed notes on the topography of the island.

In early December, changes were made in the boarding assignments. Because Komaro had taken Ganjin's party aboard, his vessel was laden far beyond its capacity. To ensure safety, some of the voyagers had to be moved onto other ships. Excepting Ganjin, Ssu-ch'a, and five others, all members of Ganjin's party were transferred to either the lead vessel or the third.

Another decision dictated the assignment of at least one speaker of Chinese to each of the three vessels. Gōgyō was ordered to move onto the second ship as a result, and Fushō onto the first. But Gōgyō was disgruntled by the arrangement. He said he would willingly be transferred to the ambassador's lead vessel, but he refused to be put aboard the second ship. He confessed to Fushō that the lead vessel, being the ambassador's, had a larger hull and was manned by more experienced seamen. If he had to change ships, he wished to be placed aboard the lead vessel.

Fushō related Gōgyō's wish to Komaro and sought his permission to exchange boarding assignments with Gōgyō. Fushō truly preferred to be aboard the second ship, for then he could be at Ganjin's side during the last few days of the homeward voyage and share with him the joy of setting foot at last on Japanese soil.

Gōgyō's changing of ships occasioned the same difficulties as at Huang-ssu-p'u. Gōgyō insisted that his scrolls also be transferred to the lead ship. As before, Fushō spoke to Komaro on Gōgyō's behalf and succeeded in having the cargo transferred. Perhaps he alone fully understood Gōgyō's obsession with the collection of scrolls.

The wind and waves fell quiet on the third of December, and total calm prevailed. The crew now awaited a favoring breeze. Toward evening on the fifth, Fushō went aboard the lead vessel to see Gōgyō. Just as he had on the third ship, Gōgyō sat near the stern, his aged body surrounded by stacks of boxes—those containing his precious scrolls.

Fushō asked Gōgyō to take a stroll with him, and together they went ashore and climbed to a high vantage point. He had wanted to speak with him once again before their departure. Gōgyō that day seemed to step out of character and become quite tractable. When they reached the summit, he muttered something about never having been there before. Fushō could not conceive of anyone, during ten tedious days of waiting in port, failing to scale this rise to view the scenery, but Gōgyō was again the exception. Gazing down at the darkening sea, he appeared pitifuly enfeebled and withered. Against this bright, expansive setting, the scars of his hardship were mercilessly revealed. Fushō saw an insignificant, crook-backed old man—distinguishable neither as a Japanese nor as a Chinese—standing alone, in the caress of the ocean breeze.

Gōgyō continued gazing at the sea as he spoke in his customary halting manner.

"I don't know what you thought of my demand, but I didn't ask to be put aboard the ambassador's ship out of

concern for my own safety. I was thinking only of the texts
I'd spent decades transcribing, that any damage or loss would
be irreparable. If anything must be taken to Japan, they must.
One can always compensate for the loss of two or three
monks, but those texts can never be replaced. Don't you
agree?"

Gōgyō rambled on in that vein. Words fell from his lips
almost inaudibly but ceaselessly, quite as if he were making
up for decades spent in silence. Since no one seemed to recognize the value of his labor, he was offering his assertion
to the heavens. His remark about the expendability of two
or three monks surely reflected his resentment at seeing the
men in Ganjin's party treated so courteously by members of
the mission, while he was not.

Fushō could not know whether Japan would benefit more
from the arrival of Ganjin than from the acquisition of an
immense quantity and variety of Buddhist texts, each of
which had been transcribed with meticulous care, word by
word, phrase by phrase. One represented the culmination of
a heroic effort that had taken two lives and exacted great
sacrifice from others over the long arduous years. The other
was the product of a lifetime of work by one man who, in
his dedication to the task, had foregone even the ordinary
human pleasures.

Fushō asked himself a question: What could this aged monk
possibly do after he got back to Japan? He had no distin-
guishing qualifications as a monk, nor did he seem to possess
authorititative knowledge of even one of the sutras. There
were no rewards awaiting him.

Gōgyō seemed to have read Fushō's thoughts. "When
those texts I've transcribed touch Japanese soil," he said,
"they'll make their own way about. They'll forsake me and
make their way everywhere. A great many monks will read
them, transcribe them, and study them. The heart of the
Buddha and his teaching will become widely known, and
correctly known. Buddhist temples will be built, and all rites
and ceremonies will flourish. There will be changes in the
appearance of monasteries, even in such details as the manner
of placing offerings on the altar."

Gōgyō was like a man possessed as he continued. "In the

main sanctuaries, in front of images of Amitābha, one will see arrays of twenty-five flowers symbolizing the twenty-five bodhisattvas. In Japan, chrysanthemums or camellias. Banners with five tassels symbolizing the Five Tathāgatas will be hung in display. Furthermore . . ."

His voice fell lower and lower and finally trailed off into inarticulate mumbling. Fushō strained to hear and was able to apprehend a few words, such as "gigaku," "sacred relic," and "sacred water," but he could not otherwise understand what the monk was trying to express. The aged Buddhist, on the threshold of his home country, seemed rapt in a state of ecstasy of his own creation.

When the sun had set, the sea breeze turned chilly, and Fushō urged that they return. They walked back to the port and parted beside the lead ship, the one on which Gōgyō would be sailing. Fushō's gaze followed Gōgyō's figure treading the plank from the dock to shipside and disappearing within.

The second vessel was moored against a bank a short distance beyond the first. As he began walking toward his own ship, Fushō awakened to the fact that he had asked Gōgyō to stroll with him but had failed to tell him any of the things he had intended to, and he felt an intense desire to see him once more. But Fushō did not turn back despite his curiosity over why the aged monk should disquiet him so.

A southerly wind arose the next morning, and the three ships set out early from the island of Okinawa, where they had been delayed for two weeks. Only moments later, however, the lead vessel ran aground on the reefs and was stuck fast. No one could estimate how long it would take to free her. There was a signal from the ambassador ordering the others to sail on. The two ships sailed past the stricken vessel and headed out toward deeper waters. Passengers and hands of the lead ship were standing on the shoal; a few dozen men were working to disengage the craft. Gōgyō would be among those stranded on the shoal, but Fushō could not detect him.

The ship on which Fushō sailed reached Yaku Island the next day, the seventh of the month. There the voyagers waited ten days for the return of favoring winds, and set sail again on the eighteenth. The nineteenth was a day of frightening turbulence. During the afternoon, the crest of a mountain was seen beyond the waves. The voyagers were told that it was probably a peak on the southern tip of Kyushu, and the reassurance came like life-giving breath. The fury continued unabated into the morning of the twentieth. Ganjin, Ssu-ch'a, and Fushō gave little thought to the possibility of the ship's foundering. They had experienced weeks of sailing through storms of much greater violence.

At dawn, Fushō was awakened by Gōgyō's shouting, which he heard while in that confused state between dream and wakefulness. The source of the shouts was obscure, but he did not doubt for a moment that it was Gōgyō calling. He saw the waves rising mightily and felt the ship being tossed about like a leaf. From brief suspension high in the foaming crests of mountainous waves, the ship would be sent plunging into cavernous valleys. Each time she glided down into these hollows, Fushō could look directly into an unnaturally clear sea, the transparent blue water revealing long undulating strands of turquoise seaweed on the ocean floor. He saw dozens of tightly wound scrolls sinking, one after another, into the deep azure—scroll after scroll, fluttering as if alive, sinking and disappearing among the undulating turquoise strands on the ocean floor. Emerging from this vision of the scrolls—from the image of scrolls sinking down and down, each following another—was the sense, a revelation perhaps, of a constant, infinite process; there was a realization of loss, of certain, irreparable loss. Each time his eyes returned to that scene, from somewhere the anguished cry of Gōgyō could be heard.

Time and again, the ship rose to mountainous heights and then pitched violently into the troughs of gigantic waves. And time and again, Fushō heard the cries of Gōgyō and saw a countless number of scrolls tumbling, sinking down into the transparent water.

Suddenly Fushō was awakened by the grip of reality. Had he been awake or dreaming? The cries of Gōgyō's desperation still rang in his ears, not as words but as mere sounds of anguish. When he closed his eyes, he envisioned the dozens, the hundreds of scrolls in leisurely descent to the turquoise entanglements; he could visualize the blue of the pellucid sea into which they were being swallowed.

His senses fully restored, Fushō looked about and saw that the ship rode easily on the undulating surface. Though the waves gathered mightily, he could sense the curious stillness that prevails when a storm is abating and the moment of peril has passed. This sea was quite unlike the sea of his vision; under the whiteness of dawn, ink-black waves rushed upon one another.

Now Fushō noticed that Ganjin, Ssu-ch'a, and Fa-chin lay supine, as if unconscious. Everyone lay in deep slumber, in utter exhaustion from two days' struggle with the raging waves.

The ship touched land that afternoon at the bay of Akimeya in the county of Ata in Satsuma Province (a fishing village in the southwestern corner of Satsuma Peninsula in Kyushu).

16

Vice-Ambassador Komaro and members of the mission who had sailed back with him set out at once from Akimeya for Dazaifu.* Fushō and the eight Chinese monks departed not long after and arrived in Dazaifu on the twenty-sixth of the month.

Setting his eyes on his homeland again after twenty years, Fushō was struck by the smallness of the natural setting. The mountains, rivers, forests, plains, and the clusters of dwellings dotting the plains—everything appeared miniature. But the sky was clear and beautiful and infinite and the atmosphere pervaded by a faint fragrance unknown on the continent.

On the eleventh of Janaury the imperial court received the formal report of Ōtomo Komaro's fulfillment of his mission to the T'ang court and arrival back in Dazaifu.

On the first day of February, Fushō arrived in Naniwa together with Ganjin's party of monks. He had set sail from that port with Yōei twenty years earlier but had returned alone. The Chinese monk Ch'ung-tao and others were at Naniwa to greet them. On the third, the party entered the province of Kawachi and was extended a formal welcome at

*The provincial headquarters, located in northern Kyushu.

the provincial office by the great councillor, Fujiwara Nakamaro, a courtier of the second rank. Among the greeters was
the monk Zendan, sent there by his teacher Tao-hsüan, who
had come from China on a ship of the previous ambassadorial mission. More than thirty other monks, including Shichū,
Kenyō, Ryōfuku, and Gyōki, were also there to comfort the
travel-weary Buddhists. The air was vibrant with the sounds
of lively commerce.

On the following day, the fourth of February, the party
left Kawachi behind them, crossed over Mount Tatsuta, and
came into the Yamato Plain. They rested briefly at the travel
station of Heguri and then pressed on, escorted by their
welcomers, toward Nara, the nation's capital.

Ganjin, Fushō, and Ssu-ch'a rode on horseback. From atop
his swaying mount, Fushō scanned the foothills lined with
monasteries: the Hōryū-ji, the Dream Hall, the Chūgū-ji
Nunnery, the Hōrin-ji, the Hokki-ji. Pagodas and halls, rising
into the clear atmosphere, lay bathed in the soft light of the
Japanese sun. The tiled roofs of Buddhist structures could be
seen amid the forests along the road leading to the capital.
Many of them had been built during Fushō's stay in the T'ang
empire.

The travelers arrived at last at the capital city of Nara, then
said to measure about two and two-third miles east to west
and almost three miles north to south. They dismounted in
front of Rashōmon, the gate at the main entrance to the capital, where they were received by the imperial emissary,
Asako-ō, a courtier of the fourth rank. They were escorted
thence to the Tōdai-ji for lodging. The monastery was
thronged with welcomers—nobles and warriors as well as
members of the clergy.

Guided by Rōben, the supervising priest of the Tōdai-ji,
the newly arrived monks walked to the Hall of the Great
Buddha and there worshipped the seated figure of Locana
Buddha, which, they were told, measured fifty-three feet in
height. The statue had been dedicated on the fourth of April,
two years before, but because the gilding was only partially
completed, it appeared unfinished. One of the tasks entrusted
to Ambassador Kiyokawa's mission, Fushō recalled, was the

purchase of gold with which this gigantic Buddha could be overlaid.

Rōben was a small man with a cold, inexpressive face. Having described the process that led to the casting of the giant image, he asked whether such a large statue of the Buddha could be found in China. "No, indeed," Ganjin replied gently. Fushō breathed easily, for the blind Ganjin could not see the statue. Of course there were no Buddhist statues of this size in China, and Fushō thought it curious that Rōben should ask the obvious.

After worshipping the Locana Buddha, the party left the Hall of the Great Buddha and were led to the guest quarters. There they were greeted by another imperial emissary who brought them consoling words acknowledging their trying experience.

The next day, they were visited by Tao-hsüan and the Brahman monk Bodhisenna, who had come together from China. Tao-hsüan had been in residence at the West T'ang Cloister of the Daian-ji since his arrival in 736 and had been lecturing on the *Sutra of Brahma's Net* and *Manual of Vinaya Sect Rituals*, thus laying the foundation for the eventual spread of *Vinaya* doctrines. The title "Teacher of the *Vinaya*" had been conferred upon him, as well as upon Ryūson, in April of 751. Tao-hsüan had taken part in the dedication of the Great Buddha of Tōdai-ji in the capacity of leader of *dhāranī* chanters. He was among the preëminent Buddhist clerics of Nara. Bodhisenna had also been in residence at the Daian-ji since his arrival in Japan and, in 752, had been awarded the exalted monastic rank of *sōjō*. He had, by imperial command, presided over the dedication of the great Buddha, and now occupied a position of leadership among the ecclesiastics of Nara.

When he met Tao-hsüan again, Fushō thought once more of the late Yōei, and of Kaiyū and Genrō, who had remained in China. Kaiyū had been the first among them to speak to Tao-hsüan about Japan, and Yōei and Fushō himself were the ones who had persuaded the distinguished Buddhist to come. Fo-t'ieh, the Annamese monk, came to them as Tao-hsüan and Bodhisenna were leaving. Fo-t'ieh had arrived in

Japan together with Tao-hsüan and had also been residing at
the Daian-ji. He, too, had participated in the dedication of
the great Buddha as a performer of the *bugaku* dances of the
continent. Many of the ranking members of the Fujiwara
family presented themselves during the day, among them,
the Minister of the Right Toyonari and the great councilor
Nakamaro.

Ganjin and members of his party devoted their first month
in Nara to meeting with visitors. Fushō was kept the busiest;
he was sought out by many who were eager to talk with
the only monk to return from among those who had sailed
with the ninth ambassadorial mission.

During the score of years he had spent away from Japan,
Fushō learned, there had been sweeping changes in politics
and Buddhism. He was astounded to learn of the change of
fortune suffered by Gembō, the learned monk who had
returned from China on a ship of the previous mission.

Upon his return to Japan Gembō's brilliance shone through
immediately, and he rose swiftly in rank to become *sōjō* in
737 and wield considerable influence among Buddhists.
Makibi, who had returned together with Gembō, was
awarded a two-step promotion to the fifth court rank within
a year of his return and, in the year following, was appointed commander of officers of the right guard. The two men,
with new knowledge from the T'ang empire, quickly became prominent in Japan's political life. But they had risen
too swiftly and had thus incurred the enmity of some of the
Fujiwaras, one of whom, Fujiwara Hirotsugu, resorted to
military action in an attempt to eliminate Gembō and Makibi.
The coup, though promptly quelled, claimed a victim. The
unfortunate Nakatomi Nashiro, former vice-ambassador to
the T'ang court, who had brought Gembō and Makibi back
to Japan, was charged with complicity and banished from
the capital. Although he was freed from exile in 741, he remained in a state of disgrace until his death four years afterward. Gembō, who had become a favorite of the Emperor,
wielded great authority for a period of ten years following
his return from China. In 745, however, he fell from grace
and was banished to the Kannon Temple in Kyushu, where
he died after a year in exile.

During the same twenty years, remarkable changes had taken place within the sphere of religion. Fushō had set out for China at a time when Japan was beset by grave social problems. Peasants were leaving the land in droves in order to evade corvée and taxation. A group of Buddhists led by Gyōgi was beginning to reach out to the common people and stimulate further unrest. The behavior of monks and nuns had fallen into extreme decadence, and the government had no means to control these followers of Buddha. Laws and regulations were wholly ineffective, and this had prompted Ryūson to turn to the T'ang empire in his search for a teacher of Buddhism who could administer monastic vows and invoke the supreme commandment of Śākya Buddha in order to chastise and reform errant Buddhists.

Gyōgi's position of authority had gradually become fortified by popular support, and the government had had no choice but to rely on him to instill order within the clergy. As a result, vagrant monks among Gyōgi's followers were able to obtain official certification of their clerical status. In 745 the government conferred the most exalted rank of dai-sōjō on Gyōgi. The popular Buddhist leader, who in earlier years had been a vitcim of the most flagrant persecution and abuse by government officials, died in 748.

Gembō and Gyōgi, the two who had risen to positions of great authority, died within a few years of each other, and, in their stead, Bodhisenna and Tao-hsüan had been elevated to prominence. The scholarly worth of the two foreign monks who came to Japan on ships of the previous mission had been duly recognized.

Indeed, the state of Buddhism in Japan had changed drastically since Fushō's departure for China. There had been a twofold purpose in Fushō and Yōei's voyage to China in search of a teacher of monastic discipline. One related to the social chaos among Buddhists in Japan—hence, one which might have been described as "political"; however, problems in that area had already been resolved. The other purpose, a purely religious one, remained to be fulfilled, for monastic vows needed to be administered and monastic discipline enforced.

17

The third ship, commanded by Vice-Ambassador Makibi, touched land on the Satsuma coast not long after the second, which had brought Fushō to the same shores. The fate of the lead vessel, with Ambassador Kiyokawa aboard, and of the fourth ship, under the command of Fusé Hitonushi, remained unknown. Whenever those who had returned safely met one another, conversations turned inevitably to concern over the fate of the missing vessels.

Even though it continued to haunt him, Fushō told no one about the disquieting vision he had experienced during his half-wakeful state that morning the ship approached the Satsuma coast. He wondered at the time whether tragedy might have befallen the lead ship. Had she foundered? Had she encountered some mishap that caused Gōgyō's scrolls to be cast into the sea? He kept silent, for his vision would be interpreted immediately as an ominous portent.

The month of February brought no news of either missing ship. In March, Kibi Makibi came to the Tōdai-ji bearing this imperial pronouncement: "You, exalted monk, came to our nation from far across the dark green sea. Indeed, my prayers have been answered, and my satisfaction knows no bounds. More than ten years ago I erected the Tōdai-ji, and it has been my wish to see an ordination platform installed there and monastic vows administered. This wish has dwelt within me constantly. My heart now rejoices, for many monks of high attainment have come from afar to transmit the codes of monasticism. I place wholly in your trust, hereafter, the administering of vows and the regulation of monasticism."

There soon followed a second pronouncement calling on Ganjin to submit the names of monks qualified to participate in the ordination rituals. Fa-chin submitted a list of names to Rōben, and soon thereafter the title "Great Teacher of the Law and Transmitter of Light" was conferred upon Ganjin, Fushō, Yen-ch'ing, T'an-ching, Ssu-ch'a, and I-ching.

On the seventeenth of March, news concerning the lead ship was received from the office of the Dazaifu in Kyushu. Investigators sent from the Dazaifu to the island of Okinawa

reported that Kiyokawa's vessel had sailed away from Okinawa for Amami Island and then was heard of no more.

At the beginning of April, an ordination platform was set
up before the Locana Buddha at the Tōdai-ji. The retired
Emperor Shōmu ascended the platform and took the Vow of
Bodhisattvas under the ministration of Ganjin, Fushō, Fa-
chin, and Ssu-ch'a. The Empress, Crown Prince, and more
than four hundred and forty members of the clergy also took
the vow. The ceremony was of unprecedented splendor.

Toward dusk, after the rituals had been concluded, Fushō
and Ssu-ch'a walked through the streets of the city, said to
have been modeled on Ch'ang-an. Cherry trees were in full
flower on the grounds of all the monasteries along the Great
Vermilion-Bird Thoroughfare. Nara lacked the gaiety of
the T'ang capital; yet many men and women strolled about
the streets, delighting in the view of the blossoms.

Passers-by frequently looked back at the pair of monks.
They regarded the Chinese monk with curiosity, so also his
Japanese companion to whom he spoke amiably in a foreign
tongue. Fushō spoke Chinese with greater facility than Japanese. He sensed that he had come to differ from his fellow
Japanese in his modes of perception and reasoning far more
than in his speech. He felt fully at ease in Ganjin's company,
and his conversations with Ssu-ch'a and Fa-chin were more
meaningful than those with his own countrymen. He and the
Chinese Buddhists had shared the same experience, all of
them having faced peril and suffering during those years of
wandering the vast continent. Their bonds were indissoluble.

Some ten days following the historic ceremony in which
an unprecedented ordination had been conferred upon the
Emperor, a report concerning the fourth ship was received
in the capital: the ship, commanded by Fusé Hitonushi, had
sailed into Ishigaki Bay in the province of Satsuma. This
joyous news revived hopes for the lead vessel.

In May, Ganjin presented the imperial court with the many
gifts he had brought from the T'ang empire — among
them, three thousand grains of the Buddha's mortal remains,
an opaline glass vase from a Western land, one bushel of
Tibetan bo-di-ci, twenty stalks of green lotus, ten pairs of

slippers from India, a scroll of calligraphy by Wang Hsi-chih, three scrolls by Wang Hsien-chih, and fifty more by other calligraphers of distinction.

Scribes at the Tōdai-ji were beginning to reproduce copies of the sacred texts that Ganjin had brought from China and presented earlier to the monastery; they were writings unknown until now in Japan. Fushō one day chanced upon the office of scribes, where the texts were being copied by a host of monks, each busily writing at his own desk. He entered the office, sat down in a corner of the room, and remained there a long while, for the scene brought back memories of Gōgyō, who had sat thus for years—hunched over his desk at the Ch'an-ting Monastery in Ch'ang-an, the Ch'an-chih Monastery in Yang-chou, the Great Fu-hsien-ssu in Lo-yang, and at a small temple near Lo-yang whose name Fushō no longer remembered.

A small inner garden was visible beyond the veranda, and a few late-blooming camellias caught Fushō's attention. Framed by the darkness within the room, the crimson camellias took on an intense brilliance. When he had last spoken with Gōgyō on the rise overlooking the island of Okinawa, Gōgyō had seemed a man possessed as he muttered halting, incoherent words about an array of twenty-five flowers symbolizing the twenty-five bodhisattvas. Fushō distinctly recalled hearing Gōgyō mention the camellia, and instantly felt the surge of a violent emotion, a mixture of grief and anger. He stood up and left the room quietly, unnoticed.

18

The fate of the lead vessel was not to be known in Japan for years to come. A report of the ship's mishap reached Ch'ang-an in the summer of 754, and Li Po on that occasion composed an elegy to Abé Nakamaro, contained in both the *Recorded Facts on T'ang Poetry* and *Complete Anthology of T'ang Poetry*:

The minister Chao of Japan leaves the imperial capital;
A solitary sail, braving the sea, circles about P'eng-lai;
The most brilliant of moons does not return,

For it has gone into the azure sea;
White clouds abound, and an air of mourning pervades
Ts'ang-wu.*

In June of 755, however, Kiyokawa and Nakamaro
returned to Ch'ang-an together with a dozen or more survivors. Their ship had been blown off course and had eventually touched land at faraway Huan-chou in Annam. Most of
the voyagers had been killed by natives or had succumbed to
disease, and only these few had survived the ordeal. Gōgyō
was not among them. Nakamaro returned to his post, and
Kiyokawa was newly appointed an official in the T'ang
administration.

The tidings concerning Kiyokawa and Nakamaro were not
to be transmitted to Japan until four years later, for shortly
after the two men had returned to Ch'ang-an, An Lu-shan
rebelled against the throne. During the great upheaval, in
756, Emperor Hsüan-tsung took to the dust-filled roads in
an escape to Ch'eng-tu, metropolis of the southwest. Com-
munication between China and Japan was suspended during
this chaotic period within the T'ang empire.

About the time Nakamaro returned to Ch'ang-an, an
ordination hall was being built in Nara on a site west of the
Hall of the Great Buddha. On the first of May of the previous
year, soon after he had taken the monastic vows, the retired
Emperor had ordered the construction of an ordination hall,
a lecture hall, monks' quarters, connecting corridors, and a
sutra repository—all according to rigid specifications—and
work was begun immediately. The Tōzen Cloister, which
was to be Ganjin's residence, was under construction across
the pond, north of the ordination hall. The ordination hall,
the first to be built in Japan, was completed in September.
Golden-bronze images of the four celestial kings were placed
in the hallowed structure. The martial figures in full armor were appropriate embellishments to the setting where

*Nakamaro was known as Chao Hen in China. P'eng-lai is a mythical
island in the eastern waters. Ts'ang-wu, perhaps best known as the name of
a plains area in central China where the legendary Emperor Shun is said to
have died, is also a conventional poetic reference to Japan.

vows of monastic discipline would be taken, and the monks of Nara beheld then with awe.

Soon after the ordination hall was dedicated, a controversy arose over Ganjin's view of ritual orthodoxy. A group of monks protested the rule requiring the presence of three masters and seven attestors at ordination rites. Insisting on the sufficiency of self-ministration of monastic vows, Kenyō, Shichū, Ryōfuku, and other monks of frugal habit and high attainment attempted to abolish the ritual newly instituted by the monk from China. The issue, it was decided, would be debated at the Hall of Vimalakīrti at the Kōfuku-ji.

Any of Ganjin's adherents could have ably argued the point of controversy. Fa-chin or Ssu-ch'a could have been effective but for the inadequacy of their Japanese. Fushō offered to represent them. Although his opponents would be Buddhist scholars of formidable attainment, Fushō felt himself possessed of an inexplicable confidence that he would triumph in this confrontation.

On the appointed day, the Hall of Vimalakīrti and the surrounding grounds were crowded with monks who had come to listen to the debate. Kenyō and his colleagues arrived at noon and seated themselves along the eastern side of the hall. Ganjin and his disciples arrived shortly thereafter and were seated opposite them. Fushō positioned himself somewhat forward, a short distance away from his colleagues. The debate began shortly. Kenyō's party proffered arguments based on the *Sutra on Divination*, whereupon Fushō asked them questions based on the "Section on Discernment," which comprised fifty-three scrolls of the *Yogācāryabhūmi Śāstra*. They did not reply. Indeed, they could not. Fushō twice urged them to respond, but no one spoke. For a short while, the hall was silent. Fushō's mind was wholly unoccupied by thought during those moments. As he sat there in the dim hall, eyes closed, he envisioned Yōei, who had expired at the Lung-hsing Monastery in far off Tuan-chou.

Not many days after the debate, Kenyō and more than eighty others forsook their previous vows and undertook monastic vows anew at the ordination hall. Kenyō, in his later life, was to attain the rank of *daisōzu*, ultimate in the

Buddhist hierarchy, to receive an imperial appointment to administer the Saidai-ji, and to serve in that position until his death at the age of seventy-nine.

Fushō's renown was greatly enhanced in consequence. He continued to reside at the Tōdai-ji and taught in the Hall of Vimalakīrti, where he lectured on the *Annotation of the Vinaya Canon* and expounded the validity of monastic regulation.

19

In February of 755, Ganjin was awarded land, which had belonged formerly to Prince Nitabé, in the western part of Nara. He wished to make it the site of a Buddhist sanctuary to be known as the "monastery where the *Vinaya* was first propagated." Although construction was suspended when the retired Emperor died, Empress Kōken willed the fulfillment of his Imperial wish and in 757 ordered the construction of a hall of worship and other buildings. The monastery was completed in August of 759. Displayed on the main gate was a gift from the Empress, a framed plate on which was inscribed the name Tōshōdai-ji, or "T'ang Buddhist Monastery." On the occasion of the dedication of the monastery, the Empress issued a rescript urging every Buddhist cleric to enter the sect of his choice only after having studied the *Vinaya* at the T'ang Monastery. Thereafter, monks from all areas converged on the monastery to hear lectures on the *Vinaya* and to receive the ministration of monastic vows.

Earlier, in July of 757, when the T'ang Monastery was still under construction, Ōtomo Komaro was charged with complicity in an unsuccessful conspiracy instigated by the minister Tachibana Naramaro and others in an attempt to manipulate the line of imperial succession; he committed suicide in prison. Such was the end that fate had deemed appropriate for the stalwart Komaro. In 758 the Japanese emissary to the kingdom of Pohai, Onu Kunitamori, returned to Japan, bringing the first news of the great rebellion in the T'ang empire. He also brought news about Kiyokawa and Nakamaro: their ship had drifted to the shores of Annam, and barely a dozen or so had survived and returned to Ch'ang-an; both Kiyokawa and Nakamaro now held offices in the T'ang government. There were no other details. The small hope

Fushō had held out for Gōgyō was extinguished. If the survivors, a scant dozen, had straggled back to Ch'ang-an with no possessions other than the clothes they wore, the aged monk could not possibly have been among them. Fushō could not conceive of Gōgyō continuing to live on, knowing that his scrolls had been lost.

On the day he received this news, Fushō conducted memorial rites for Gōgyō and, as a personal remembrance, he considered planting a fruit-bearing tree somewhere by the side of a road outside the city. Then he recalled the rows of elms that lined the nine avenues and twelve boulevards of Ch'ang-an and wished he could provide the people of Nara with the pleasure of seeing luxuriant summer foliage and autumnal fruit along the streets of their own city. His wish was soon to be fulfilled. His request was submitted and approved in June, and during the remainder of the year he devoted his leisure to the work of planting.

The return of the Japanese emissary from Pohai had put an end to the hope Fushō held out for Gōgyō's return. The event had a further particular meaning for Fushō, for the emissary had been entrusted with a huge roof tile to be delivered to him. It was addressed to "Fushō, Buddhist monk of Japan," but Fushō's inquiries revealed only that the roof tile had been sent from China through Pohai for delivery in Japan. He could not learn the identity of the sender.

The tile was a *shibi*,* which, paired with its like, arches skyward at the end of the roof ridge of a Buddhist temple. Evidently of great age, the *shibi* was chipped in many places and had a crevice across the length of its surface. Fushō had a vague recollection of the form. He had undoubtedly seen it somewhere in the T'ang empire. He might have seen it at the Great Fu-hsien Monastery in Lo-yang, where he had spent more than two years following his arrival in China, or possibly at the Ch'ung-fu-ssu, which was his residence over a considerable period of time in Ch'ang-an, or at the King Aśoka Monastery in Mou-shan. Though he could recall it only hazily, he was certain of its being an object he had seen often.

Shibi referred originally to the tail of a gigantic mythical creature of the sea .

Fushō was puzzled. A Chinese would hardly have bothered to send such an artifact. The only Japanese in China with whom he had been intimate were Genrō and Kaiyū. Nevertheless, Fushō regarded with some awe the curiously shaped roof tile that had come from China, a nation now torn by rebellion, had crossed the land of Pohai, and then the sea, to be delivered to him in Japan. He placed the aged *shibi* beside the entrance of his quarters at the Tōdai-ji. Three months later he presented it to Fujiwara Takafusa, who was then overseeing the construction of the T'ang Buddhist Monastery.

The principal edifices of the T'ang Buddhist Monastery were completed in August of 759. Whenever Fushō entered the grounds of the monastery, he never failed to lift his eyes to the roof of the Hall of Worship. There, arching gracefully from the ends of the ridge piece, were two *shibi*, cast in a form identical to the Chinese roof tile he had presented to Takafusa.

Epilogue

In February of 760, Bodhisenna died after pronouncing his final admonitions to his disciples and invoking Amitābha; he was fifty-six. Not long after Bodhisenna's death, in April, Tao-hsüan died at the age of fifty-eight. Makibi, who had been an intimate of Tao-hsüan, wrote an account of the late monk's accomplishments; taken from that account for inclusion in Saichō's ninth-century compilation, *The Lineage of Transmitters of the Buddhist Law*, was the following passage: "The exalted monk constantly recited passages from the *Sutra of Brahma's Net*. During the solemn recitations, his voice rang clear, like jade, and yet like metal. It had the effect of engendering goodness in people; it was both melodious and mysterious. He was well versed in the *Vinaya* scriptures and profound in his grasp of the doctrine of Zen." Tao-hsüan in later times came to be regarded as the original transmitter to Japan of the Kegon doctrine, and the second in the line of transmitters of Zen. Ryūson died on the very day of Tao-hsüan's death. He had initiated the search for teachers of monastic discipline and had sent Fushō and Yōei to China in their quest.

Ganjin died in the spring of 763, four years after the construction of the T'ang Buddhist Monastery. His disciple Ninki dreamed one night that the main beam of the lecture hall collapsed. Interpreting this as a manifestation of the venerable monk's wish to be delivered of earthly existence, he gathered together the many disciples of Ganjin, and they had a life portraiture made of the exalted monk. Ganjin died on the sixth of May; he was seventy-five. He was seated in the pose of the Tathāgata and facing westward in the last moments of his life. A touch of warmth lingered in his forehead for three days after his expiration. For this reason his funeral could not be conducted until some time later.

In the year following Ganjin's death, the imperial court dispatched emissaries to the many monasteries of Yang-chou. At every monastery, monks donned mourning robes, and for three days sent their prayers eastward to Japan. At the Lung-hsing Monastery a great religious feast was held in his memory. Some years later, the Lung-hsing Monastery was leveled by a conflagration that spared only the building in which Ganjin had resided.

During that same year, 764, the Korean kingdom of Silla sent an envoy, Kim Se-bu, to Japan. The envoy inquired about the Japanese student-monk Kaiyū in the hope of finding out whether or not he had returned to Japan, for he was known to have left China on a homeward journey to Japan by way of Pohai. Kim had been asked to verify Kaiyū's return by the T'ang Imperial Emissary to Silla, Han Ch'ao-ts'ai, who had traveled through Pohai on his way to the kingdom of Silla. Their interest suggests that Kaiyū, though he had sworn never again to set foot in his native country, may have disavowed that intent and returned to Japan. This becomes more than conjecture in the light of a single piece of documentary evidence. It is recorded in an ancient chronicle that a monk named Kaiyū and his lay servant boarded a ship carrying a T'ang emissary to Pohai, and then sailed from Pohai to Japan; and that the shipmaster cast this lay servant overboard when the ship sailed into a storm.

The year of Fushō's death is not known. He may not have lived to receive these tidings of Kaiyū. Had he been alive, Fushō would then have been close to sixty years of age.